BRIDE'S
NEW WAYS
TO WED

BRIDE'S
NEW WAYS
TO WED

A GUIDE TO PERSONALIZING YOUR WEDDING

The Editors of
BRIDE'S Magazine
with
Antonia van der Meer

A Perigee Book

Perigee Books
are published by
The Putnam Publishing Group
200 Madison Avenue
New York, NY 10016

Library of Congress Cataloging-in-Publication Data

Bride's new ways to wed: a guide to personalizing your wedding/
the editors of *Bride's* magazine with Antonia van der Meer.
    p. cm.
    ISBN 0-399-51575-5
    1. Wedding etiquette. I. Van der Meer, Antonia. II. *Bride's*
magazine.
    HQ745.B79   1990   89-39073 CIP
395'.22—dc20

Printed in the United States of America
1 2 3 4 5 6 7 8 9 10

ACKNOWLEDGMENTS

BRIDE'S magazine would like to thank the following editorial staff members—daily in touch with the new ways that couples across the country are getting married. Their reporting, and visions, have shaped this book. . . .

Editor-in-Chief Barbara D. Tober, who inspired each contributor; Managing Editor Andrea Feld, who guided the efforts; and staff editors Tamara Eberlein, Heather Twidale, Julia Martin, and Robyn Liverant.

Special thanks to Phyllis Richmond Cox, for her artistic contributions to the cover, and to Millie Martini Bratten, Sally Kilbridge, and Cynthia Penney.

Contents

Foreword

This very special book is dedicated to a very special couple: the bride and groom who want a beautiful, personal ceremony that reflects their style. As *individuals* in today's "cookie cutter" society, you and your groom seek to make a statement to your family and friends about yourselves, your love, and your future. You are proud to be *individuals*, first and foremost, joining together in friendship and partnership. For you, the wedding celebration must reflect your hopes and heritage, your joy and seriousness of purpose, the magic you find in each other.

What *are* these *New Ways to Wed,* and how are they different from the traditions of the past? These are celebrations that speak to the needs and wishes of people marrying in the 1990s: couples who are older, who often live far from home, who study, work, travel, and intend to continue this pattern all the days of their lives. *New Ways to Wed* are Long Weekend Weddings that invite generations of relatives and friends from many miles away to festivities lasting three, four, even five days. The meeting place may be the bride's or the groom's hometown; or everyone may take a Sentimental Journey to a favorite family vacation spot or other significant place for a weekend of nostalgia. If the clan can't travel, then the bride and groom will fly or drive to *her* home, then *his* home, and finally to their honey-moon destination to complete a Progressive Wedding. Or . . . they may choose to invite guests to join them in an exotic locale for a few days of partying—a Honeymoon Wedding. And if only the bride and groom know they're going to a wedding, but the guests haven't a clue, *everyone* is bound to have the Surprise Wedding of their lives.

Included, too, are complete instructions for planning a Long-Distance Wedding, as well as information on having a pastoral Day in the Country or a glamorous Wedding Day on the Ocean. Medieval weddings, complete with jousting matches; Renaissance, Victorian, and other period weddings enhanced by old-world flowers, theme music and dancing, historic cakes and toasts of the times, are described in depth. There are hundreds of wedding ideas to inspire you to create your *own* themes—traditions that will be distinctly *yours* and will go down in the history of your family as Heirlooms for future generations.

Although weddings come in all sizes and prices, *creativity*—not the amount of money spent—is the essential factor. Yes, there is a chapter on the Ultimate Wedding, with extravagant examples of fantasies and dreams come true—for equally extravagant costs. But the essence of each successful wedding celebration, we have found, is *the combination of personal touches* from both bride and groom that make this "Rite of Passage" unique.

And now . . . enjoy the search for *your* perfect wedding day theme. The excitement begins on page one, and your celebration can only be equal to your sense of adventure.

BARBARA TOBER
Editor-in-Chief
BRIDE'S magazine

1.
Which Wedding Style Suits You?

Brides and grooms are blazing new trails, experimenting with creative wedding themes, saying "I do" in different locations, giving a fresh twist to old traditions, pioneering innovative ceremonies and receptions. After a beautiful and solemn wedding ceremony, the reception—which is a party that joins you and your two families—can incorporate the backgrounds and life-styles that make you and your groom special as a couple.

With so many choices in wedding styles today, your opportunities for finding the style of wedding that is right for you are multiplied by your imagination. Everyone wants this day to be perfect. The marriage day reflects not only tradition but also the individual tastes and styles of the couple and their families. Even couples who start out thinking that they don't want to make a big fuss over their wedding, such as couples marrying for the second time, often end up choosing a large, traditional wedding or a lavishly creative celebration. Brides and grooms—and their families—are celebrating like never before. With so many choices out there, your biggest problem will be deciding which style of wedding is right for you.

To help you decide what type of wedding might suit you best, take the quiz below and start to think about your options. The quiz should help you to create the wedding event that matches your style. Remember, brides and their mothers are no longer alone in the decision making. You will want to discuss this quiz and your answers with your fiancé, and with both sets of parents. The two families, together, are often very involved in the wedding these days—both financially and emotionally. Make everyone feel an integral part of your day by including them in wedding decisions, asking for their opinions, incorporating their family traditions, and taking their advice where appropriate.

Section I: ABOUT YOURSELVES

1. You and your fiancé:
   a. come from the same hometown.
   b. come from nearby cities.
   c. come from opposite ends of the country or even the world.

2. Your family:
   a. is spread out all over the country.
   b. lives in or near the same town.
   c. lives outside the U.S.

3. Your groom's family:
   a. is spread out all over the country.
   b. lives in or near the same town.
   c. lives outside the U.S.

4. The following statement applies:
   a. My groom and I have never been married before.
   b. We have both been married before.
   c. One of us was married before.

5. The following statement applies:
   a. My groom and I both have children.
   b. We have no children.
   c. One of us has children.

Section II: WEDDING IDEAS

1. The ideal wedding size is:
   a. large, with 200 or more guests.
   b. medium, around 80 to 200 guests.
   c. small, fewer than 80 guests.

2. I want my wedding to be:
    a. formal and steeped in tradition.
    b. grand and festive but stamped with personal style.
    c. low-key and informal, an intimate celebration.

3. I think I would look and feel best in:
    a. a long gown and cathedral veil.
    b. a floor-length dress with a veil, hat, or floral wreath.
    c. a knee-length dress or suit.

4. Wedding guests should receive invitations:
    a. engraved on ivory parchment with traditional wording.
    b. engraved or printed with personalized wording, perhaps accompanied by a cartoon, illustration, or photograph.
    c. written or delivered by hand, maybe even faxed!

5. Receptions are most fun when:
    a. lavish, with a three-course seated dinner and dancing to a big band.
    b. festive but unusual, with reggae music, fireworks, boat rides, or a hot-air balloon getaway for bride and groom.
    c. informal and lively, with square dancing and a barbecue or picnic.

Section III: NEW WAYS TO WED

Check as many as you like.
1. I have always considered myself:
    a. a traditionalist; I imagine myself as an all-in-white bride at a big wedding with all the trimmings and customs.
    b. a little different from the crowd; I might want a religious ceremony and seated dinner, but I might also wear a short wedding dress, write my own vows.
    c. a trailblazer who isn't afraid to depart from the standard; I can see myself in an eyelet lace or Western-style dress, marrying outside

the horse ranch where I spend most of my leisure time.

2. If I decided to break from tradition, I would:
   a. marry in an unusual spot—on the beach, in a cave, atop a mountain.
   b. make a dramatic statement—choose black velvet dresses for my maids, march down the aisle alone, drive away from the wedding on a motorcycle with a white leather jacket thrown over my gown.
   c. add a personal touch—unusual ethnic customs, a chocolate wedding cake, a song I wrote myself.

3. My fiancé and I want to personalize our wedding by:
   a. reflecting our hobbies (for example, exchange our vows on a boat if we're both sailors).
   b. making a statement about the way we met or fell in love (for example, tie the knot at the chapel on the college campus where we first met).
   c. using a theme we think would be fun for guests (for example, throw a period celebration with historic costumes, jousting contests, minstrels).

4. When it comes to wedding taboos and traditions, I think:
   a. it's okay for the groom to see the bride in her gown right before the wedding.
   b. it isn't necessary to marry in a church or synagogue.
   c. it would be fun to stay on after the wedding reception to continue partying with friends and family the next day.

5. My dream wedding would take place:
   a. over a long weekend, with a series of parties, picnics, sports events, and dinners.
   b. over the course of one fabulously extravagant day.
   c. while on vacation with family and friends in a beautiful and romantic spot.

This quiz will get you thinking and talking about your wedding plans, something you should continue to do as you read further in this book and get more fabulous ideas for celebrations. Now, here's a clearer look at the quiz.

Section I

Give some thought to the basics in your life first. Do all your fiancé's relatives and old school friends live in England? Then, you may want to forgo a traditional hometown wedding celebration in favor of a Honeymoon Wedding in London. Or consider a Progressive Wedding, where you marry here, then travel to England for a second formal celebration in your honor thrown by the groom's side of the family. (See Chapter Four, "Travel Weddings.")

Are all your relatives and friends scattered across the country? A reunion combined with a Long Weekend Wedding may be in order. Three days give family and friends—and you—plenty of time to get back in touch with one another. (See Chapter Three, "The Long Weekend Wedding.") Do you and your groom currently live in different cities? How will you coordinate wedding plans? (See the section on long-distance wedding planning, Chapter Four.) Where will you marry if everyone resides in a different city? Maybe you'd prefer to opt for neutral ground in a beautiful location: a Honeymoon Wedding.

Is this the second marriage for one or both of you? If so, you might want to do things a little differently this time. Perhaps a Surprise Wedding is for you (see Chapter Six). On the other hand, you may now have the ways and means to throw the ultraformal, supersophisticated wedding party you've always dreamed of. (See Chapter Five, "Ultimate Weddings," for fantasy ideas.)

Section II

This section helps identify the wedding style of your choice. A predominance of A answers indicates a desire for a formal, traditional wedding. A majority of B answers shows an inclination toward uniquely elegant celebrations. A preference for C answers is a clue that you lean toward more intimate, informal parties. As you take the quiz, you may discover some surprising things about yourself and your groom. Perhaps you thought you'd prefer an informal celebration, but now find yourself dreaming of cathedral trains and organs playing Handel. Traditional weddings with all the trimmings are very much in fashion. But the traditional weddings of the 1990s are, at the same time, very personal. Couples today want their weddings to make a statement about themselves, their life-styles, their relationships.

Section III

New types of weddings have emerged as couples are finding fewer rigid rules and more options available to them. This section should help you think about ways to personalize your wedding. Don't back away from including the unusual. What do you fancy? A backless wedding dress to show off your tan at a summer wedding? A carrot cake at the reception for a nutrition-conscious bride? A bouquet of red roses because they mean "I love you"? A special song sung because you heard it on your first date? Cajun food to recall your early years in New Orleans? These things make today's weddings even more special, and they have spawned some of the newest trends in weddings: Long Weekend Weddings; Progressive Weddings (the couple visits and celebrates with family and friends across the country or even the world); Sentimental Journey Weddings (the couple returns to a spot, such as a college campus, imbued with meaning); Honeymoon Weddings; Ultimate Weddings; and Theme Weddings (in period costume, in the country, on the water). So take your time and stretch your imagination. With ingenuity, planning, and good taste, your fantasy wedding can become a reality.

2.
The New Etiquette

Wedding celebrations have become increasingly personal these days, with myriad possibilities for marrying and partying, leading to a potpourri of themes and styles. Wedding customs, attitudes, and etiquette, not surprisingly, have changed along with the ways we wed. The new etiquette balances your needs and wants with tradition, consideration for others, and good taste. A wedding celebration is as much for family and friends as it is for you. In this chapter, you'll find out all about the etiquette of invitations and receiving lines, transportation and flowers, wedding gifts and good-byes. Independent-minded couples can stretch the rules as they add their own personal touches to their weddings, as long as they use common sense and make courteous, thoughtful requests.

Finances

Almost before you do anything else, you must sit down and determine how much money can be spent on the wedding and reception plus any additional parties. New-style weddings call for new-style financing that often involves many more people than the bride's parents. The new etiquette for this situation calls for early and honest talks about money matters. Everyone—the bride, the groom, and both sets of parents (but not necessarily all at the same time)—should be involved in this discussion.

Much of the style of your day, including the food, music, number of guests, and site of the wedding, will depend on what you are willing to spend. Can you afford the Ultimate Wedding you dream of, complete with thirty-three-piece orchestra, fireworks, and a seated dinner for five hundred? If you had to cut down on one aspect of your dream wedding, what would it be: the number of people you wanted to invite or the poached salmon and imported truffles you wanted to serve? Will a Long Weekend Wedding be expensive or are friends and relatives eager to host a picnic, a pool party, and a luncheon in your honor? Are there many important family members who won't be able to travel to the wedding due to distance? Should you consider bringing the wedding to them? How would that change the costs? Which of your family members and friends could pay for airline tickets and hotel rooms to watch you wed at a honeymoon location? What would a Honeymoon Wedding cost?

These tips should help you conquer any financial worries or disagreements:

• Keep financial talks straightforward and clear.

• Create a line-by-line budget with separate listings for all your expenses—from wedding dress to champagne.

• Show a spirit of compromise if financial talks get tense. You don't want to fight out every detail with your parents or soon-to-be in-laws.

• Decide who will pay—the bride and groom, the bride's family, or a combination. Some couples these days want to (or must) shoulder part or all of the cost of the wedding themselves. If your parents are having trouble paying for your dream wedding, you might compromise and offer to split costs while assuring them that they'll still be the official "hosts" of the day. More often, the bride's parents still pay for most or all of the festivities. With increasing frequency, however, the groom's parents are pitching in as well, making this a party that truly joins two families.

• When costs are split between families, avoid any

awkward moments by simply assigning each family specific expenses. For example, the groom's family might agree to pay for flowers, limousine, church fees, and liquor, while the bride's parents pay for food, wedding dress, music, and site rental.

• Let the groom deal with his own parents if sticky situations arise. If financial involvement on the part of the groom's parents leads to the feeling that they're running the show, the groom is in the best position to convince them that your original wedding plans should be respected.

Scheduling

When choosing a date for your wedding, keep in mind not only your own preferences but those of your guests. Scheduling a wedding in the middle of a holiday weekend, for example, may present a problem for guests who like to take advantage of long weekends by going away. Such a date *can* work, however, if you entertain guests throughout the weekend. Three days of parties allow guests time to meet new friends and greet old ones. When determining the date and time of your wedding, don't overlook religious observances, local customs, and the degree of wedding formality. Take practical information into consideration. For example, since June is the most popular wedding month, you may find that your wedding conflicts with others, making caterers and reception sites hard to book. Friends may have other commitments as well. A winter month, on the other hand, may be the perfect time to entice friends and family down to Jamaica or another hot spot for a Honeymoon Wedding. Check for a week convenient to those closest to you before making arrangements. For close friends or siblings who have children, keep school vacations in mind. Make it easy for loved ones to join you.

Sites

Under water, or mountaintops, behind waterfalls, on the beach, in an airplane, on a baseball diamond . . . these are but a few of the untraditional spots where couples choose to marry. There are so many options, so many different sites where brides and grooms tie the knot or celebrate afterward. Your quest may even lead you to the Official Center of the World, which happens to be in Felicity, California. Couples can marry at the marble pyramid commemorating the center and for a few moments, at least, the world will literally revolve around them! With a little thought and investigative work, that dream location can be yours. Why not an art gallery? A yacht? A historic mansion? An old barn? One couple married on a Ferris wheel . . . another on a roller coaster. If this seems too adventurous, think of ways to personalize a more traditional site. A hotel ballroom can sparkle with your personal touch if you add rented trees, shrubs, floral centerpieces, and special lighting. Let your creativity and sentiments run wild when choosing a site, but do not forget budget constraints. Stretch your imagination by flipping through the yellow pages, asking friends for their thoughts, or driving around town in search of ideas and interesting locations. Consider your favorite hobbies. (For more on fabulous or off-beat sites, see Chapter Five, "Ultimate Weddings.")

When choosing a site, be sure to keep these things in mind:

- the number of guests you plan to invite
- the type of reception you hope to have (dancing, buffet or seated dinner, etc.)
- the available dates
- the number of people who can be accommodated
- fees, deposits, overtime charges
- any special rules or regulations that may affect the party (Speak with the banquet manager, catering manager, or whoever will be in charge at the time of your wedding.)
- practical issues (For example, an outdoor wedding may be a breath of fresh air for you, but if it comes complete with insects or a downpour, everyone will be uncomfortable. You can prepare for these possibilities by prespraying with insecticide or lighting punk sticks or citronella candles. Anticipate the possibility of rain by renting a tent, set up three days ahead of time so the ground is dry. Or plan to have a backup indoor site.)

- accessibility of site to disabled guests
- distance between church or synagogue and reception site
- hours the site is available for use
- choice of caterer (Some sites may demand a certain caterer be used. Others leave the choice up to you.)
- restaurant facilities on site (Some places have only a warming area, and food cannot actually be cooked there.)

Creative Invitations

One couple, who met while acting, sent invitations that read "The show you've been waiting for—one performance only!" True to the theme of their invitations, the couple married onstage against a backdrop of a curtain adorned with theatrical comedy/tragedy masks. Another couple printed their silhouettes in black on a white invitation. Yet another sent guests a cartoon strip of their courtship done by a local artist. Two magazine editors sent out a humorous, copy-edited wedding invitation, complete with red pencil "corrections" and comments above the traditional wording.

Your invitations can be as expressive of your style as the rest of your wedding. They should complement your wedding style and act as a precursor of the wedding festivities to come. Here's how:

- If your wedding signifies the marriage of many backgrounds, a *multilingual invitation* may say it all for you. Translate the wording of the invitation into Swedish, Greek, Japanese—whatever language suits. Place the translation on facing pages or print the foreign language invitation on an insert. Foreign guests will feel especially welcome.
- For a *country wedding*, invitations can be pressed with leaves or butterflies.
- Invitations can be scrolled or hand printed in calligraphy for a *period celebration*.
- Couples who opt for more *traditional weddings* usually want a traditional invitation. Rich ivory paper formally engraved with traditional wording would be a good match for this type of wedding.
- For a *Victorian-style wedding*, an invitation with

Old English wording and trimmed with a burgundy velvet ribbon would be a dramatic choice.

• For an *Art Deco celebration*, the cool, sophisticated look of black, silver, and gold lettering will surprise and delight guests.

• *A New Year's Eve wedding* might call for an invitation sprinkled with colored, sparkling confetti.

• *Small weddings* lend themselves to more informal, intimate invitations, such as handwritten or hand-delivered notes.

• *A Long Weekend Wedding*, with its progression of parties, deserves an invitational package complete with the wedding invitation and listings of all the other events, maps, and locations.

• *A Theme Wedding* should be announced in keeping with the style for the day: thread silver and black ribbons through a Halloween invitation or shape the invitations like hearts for Valentine's Day.

• *A Honeymoon Wedding* invitation will surely intrigue and entice guests if it includes a pen-and-ink illustration of the romantic site you've chosen (swaying palm trees on a Hawaiian beach? the Manhattan skyline?).

• If you are having a *Progressive Wedding*, which moves from town to city with, for example, a party given by the bride's parents in New York followed by a party thrown by the groom's grandparents in Boca Raton, Florida, each party deserves its own special invitation. The wording for the after-wedding party can be just as formal as a traditional wedding invitation. The invitation from the parents of the groom might read "Mr. and Mrs. Charles Smith/request the pleasure of your company/at a reception in honour of/Mr. and Mrs. Thomas Smith/Sunday, the fourteenth of July/three o'clock/at Sea Winds Inn/Boca Raton, Florida."

Once you have some ideas, speak with a printer or engraver. If you want to reproduce a special photo or illustration (even a cartoon) for the invitation, the printer will be able to tell you how well it will reproduce and what it will cost. A calligrapher can create a prototype for a "handwritten" invitation, which can then be copied by a printer or engraver.

No matter what your invitation style, be sure to

give guests plenty of time to schedule your wedding day into their plans. Send invitations about a month in advance of the day. Invitations should go out even *earlier* if the celebration occurs over a long weekend or at a honeymoon location. Even before you mail the official invitation, call key people with news of your wedding and the date. To get the word out early to everyone on your guest list, perhaps send an informal announcement, promising more details and invitations later. Order invitations at least three months in advance, allowing four weeks or more for printing. Be sure to proofread every word when you pick them up. You don't want any mistakes. Start addressing envelopes as soon as you have them. This task can take longer than you think and you'll want to be ready to send them out on time. For more information on the etiquette of invitations, see *BRIDE'S Book of Etiquette*.

Wedding Attire

Today's bridal selections are varied. There are looks and styles to fit every height, figure, and personality. Actress Heather Locklear wore a strapless, form-fitting, mermaid-style wedding dress to her wedding. Model Elle Macpherson wore a backless, partly transparent wedding dress designed by Azzedine Alaïa. Such styles, however, are not limited to celebrities. Any bride can don a dress as dramatic and revealing as theirs (or one that's elegant and demure).

There are many dress styles to choose from with cathedral, chapel, or sweep trains; floor-, knee-, or ankle-length hems; handkerchief points; or bustles. Fashion options include street-length suits or backless gowns, all with jackets—for the ceremony. Brides today—both first- and second-time—are stretching the rules and wearing soft pastels and fashionable styles that express their personalities. Brides now dress in living color, with underskirts, sashes, reembroidered flowers, and other trimmings in color, and for the boldest stroke even scarlet wedding dresses! A soap opera wedding, in which the TV bride wore a black-and-white wedding dress, prompted a flood of calls and letters from women who wanted to know where a gown just like it could be found for their weddings. Black, a color that can definitely be worn again, is a popular choice in combination with white or other colors for bridesmaids at a city or hotel wedding.

At one traditional wedding, the bride, groom, and bridal party all wore dark sunglasses for an eccentric effect. Another bride sported a short white motorcycle jacket over her formal white gown. Brides who will feel comfortable in something traditional at the ceremony but want something more expressive afterward are choosing gowns with long skirts that can be removed, revealing shorter dresses beneath for dancing at the reception. One bride wore a long skirt with a chapel-length train and matching jacket with a Queen Anne collar during the ceremony. At the reception she whisked off the jacket to reveal a daring satin bustier.

The bride's dress, the groom's outfit, and the bridal party's attire will help set the tone of your wedding. The bride may fall in love with a certain gown and plan her wedding around it, or she may have a particular theme or wedding style in mind and shop for a dress to match. For example, to complement a wedding theme of winter wonderland, a bride might choose a white velvet dress. Fur trim could be a dramatic enhancement at a formal winter wedding. Some December/January brides wear elegant capes lined with fur, velvet, or wool. Other seasons and themes call for different outfits. One bride, at a country wedding in Vermont, wore a calico dress with three petticoats beneath. A bride in the Southwest added ornately stitched white cowboy boots to her white, fringed suede wedding day attire. Her groom wore a tuxedo—and a cowboy hat.

For second weddings, bridal dress options are equally unlimited. The bride can choose from among the same dresses and gowns that delight a first-time bride: from a body-revealing, strapless, satin and lace sheath, to a full-skirted ball gown, to a wedding suit—in white linen or lace with a feminine jacket and a narrow skirt. Many bridal suits have dressy additions—such as rhinestone buttons, ruffles, pleats, or hem stitching and the like on the jacket.

(Norma Kamali, for example, designs a white-and-gold embroidered silk suit with a vest that's perfect for second-time brides who want a nontraditional but dramatic bridal outfit.) For long gowns, the trend today is toward simple elegance, a sculptural cut with an evening wear influence. A veil (an age-old symbol of virginity) and a train (synonymous with the larger-than-life aura of a first-time bride) are not usually recommended for a woman who has been married before.

Many choices exist for the men in the wedding party as well, from white tie to the white leather tuxedo worn by Heather Locklear's groom. The groom might choose polka-dot suspenders, or a paisley cummerbund and matching bow tie, or accessories that match the color chosen for the bridesmaids. At one wedding, all the ushers wore lavender cummerbunds, the bride's favorite color. An iconoclastic groom wore a black silk shirt under his tuxedo. At a nautical theme wedding aboard a paddle ship, the groom dressed as a ship's captain. Although it's best if the groom's outfit complements that of the bride, this rule can be broken. Some grooms have selected pastel dinner jackets over plaid pants for an informal ceremony. Edwin Schlossberg sported a Willi Smith suit with baggy pants and a silver tie when he married Caroline Kennedy, who wore a formal and traditional wedding dress.

Traditionally, a man would wear a black or dark gray cutaway with gray-and-black striped trousers for a very formal daytime wedding. After six o'clock, white tie is *de rigueur*. (Select the style of dress according to the time of the ceremony, not the time of the reception.) At a semiformal or informal wedding, dark suits and neckties are appropriate. The groom, ushers, and both fathers traditionally wear the same outfits. The groom may distinguish himself from the other men either with different formal wear altogether (cutaway to their stroller; tails to their tuxedo) or by varying his accessories or boutonniere. The father of the groom might also want to dress in an outfit similar to that worn by the ushers and father of the bride, but it is not required.

Children's clothes can be traditional or wildly creative. Sailor suits, all-white linen outfits, shorts and knee socks, tiny tuxedos and child-size dresses in the fabric of the maids' dresses are popular choices. One couple with a teddy bear theme dressed their little ring "bear-er" in an adorable bear costume.

Guests dress according to the time of day and degree of formality your invitation heralds. Some brides and grooms today specify a dress code for guests in keeping with their wedding style. For example, when actor Stacy Keach married Polish-born actress Malgosia Romassi, they asked that their two hundred guests all wear white. At a period wedding held at a Renaissance fair, one bride suggested that guests join the fun by coming in Renaissance attire. Guests might also be asked to wear turn-of-the-century outfits to a Victorian garden party or to bring stylized masks to a Halloween wedding.

Choosing Attendants

Much will depend on the size and formality of your wedding. You may choose to have only two attendants at your wedding or as many as twelve bridesmaids and twelve groomsmen. Or you could have an unequal number of male and female attendants. Maids traditionally take part in the wedding day procession and stand by your side at the ceremony, next to the groom in the receiving line. Ushers seat the guests, act as escorts for the bridesmaids, and stand by the groom's side at the wedding (but are not usually in the receiving line). All attendants usually sit at the bridal table at the reception.

Although attendants are usually friends or relatives of the same sex and age as the bride or groom, this need not be the case. Here are some choices:

• In the South, a groom traditionally chooses his father to be his best man.

• An actress of the TV show "St. Elsewhere" asked her eighty-six-year-old grandmother to be her matron of honor.

• The sex of the attendants can be mixed and matched. The bride might choose her best friend to be a "man of honor" instead of a maid of honor, or the groom might appoint a "best woman" instead of a best man. (Or call an honor attendant "best person.'') This is an excellent way to honor a best friend who happens to be a member of the opposite sex.

• Pets can play a role. One bride decorated her beloved Labrador retriever with a flowered collar and included him in the procession. It's a good idea, however, to hire a trainer if you want your pet to be part of the wedding day.

• Children are a charming addition to the wedding party as pages, ring bearers, or flower girls, and they represent the generations in a joyous family celebration. A ring bearer can be a girl or a boy. (A child should not carry the real things, however; give them to your honor attendants.) A shy tot can be escorted down the aisle by another, older child. If your heart is set on child attendants, be sure you've taken their bedtimes into consideration. A late evening wedding may strain the good nature of the most even-tempered youngster.

Music

From the regal sounds of a thirteen-piece orchestra to the majesty of trumpets, brides and grooms are choosing music with individual flair. A guitar player may strum such meaningful favorites as ''Evergreen,'' or there may be strains of chamber music in the air.

No matter what your style of wedding, music can add to the mood of the moment. Ceremony music can reflect your taste, from country/Western tunes and top-forty songs to a harp and flute combination playing classical music. Check with your house of worship first, however. It may allow only religious music. Listen to many types of music before making your selection. For a traditional ceremony at a church, chapel, or synagogue, the music may be a majestic organ or trumpet. But when it comes to music, you can pull out all the stops for a big, formal wedding. To personalize the ceremony further, have a friend or family member with musical talent sing or play an instrument. One bride's aunt sang an old Italian love song, which added both a personal and an ethnic touch to the ceremony.

Reception music can range from a pianist or a

SONGS FOR THE WEDDING

Here is a mix of traditional and untraditional tunes that couples are requesting:

Processional/Recessional

"Theme from *Chariots of Fire,*" by Vangelis

"*Canon in D Minor,*" by Pachelbel

"*Nadia's Theme*" from
The Young and the Restless,
performed by Barry de Vorzon and
Perry Botkin, Jr.

"*Trumpet Voluntary,*" by Clarke

"*Water Music,*" by Handel

Ceremony

"*Always and Forever Amen,*"
sung by Randy Travis

"*Evergreen,*" sung by Barbra Streisand

"*Jesu, Joy of Man's Desiring,*" by Bach

"*Sunrise/Sunset*" from *Fiddler on the Roof,*
by Harnick, Bock

"*The Lord's Prayer,*" by Malotte

wind ensemble to the big-band sound or a DJ spinning records and tapes. Dancing is not a must, but it does add to the fun, and many people expect it. And it gives everyone the chance to loosen up and let go of their inhibitions. One couple chose two bands to play at their traditional outdoor wedding. Bridesmaids in pink taffeta danced first to the standard big-band sound, later to a rollicking reggae band. Another couple wanted to bring southwestern touches to their wedding day and chose Mexican mariachi music to enhance the flavor of the wedding (which also included six-foot-high cacti, votive candles, and a wedding cake shaped like an adobe house). Motown music is popular, as well as hit tunes from movies like *Dirty Dancing*. Songs can be tied to your theme or personal interests. A couple

CROWD PLEASERS AT THE RECEPTION

"Celebration," sung by Kool & The Gang

"I Heard It Through the Grapevine,"
sung by Marvin Gaye

"La Bamba," sung by Richie Valens
or Los Lobos

"Mony Mony," sung by Tommy James
and The Shandells

"Pink Cadillac,"
sung by Bruce Springsteen or Natalie Cole

"Shout," sung by Otis Day & The Knights

"Twist and Shout," sung by The Isley Brothers

planning to honeymoon in Paris, for example, might ask the band to play "I Love Paris."

If your backgrounds are ethnically diverse, don't overlook the music of your heritage. Couples have hired Scottish bagpipe players, Czechoslovakian folk dancers, a trio of Hawaiian ukulele players, and Middle Eastern belly dancers! At a Jewish wedding, "Hava Nagila" is always popular. At Italian weddings, bands play the tarantella. At Polish weddings, polkas are requested. Some couples take dance lessons before their weddings—in anticipation of these ethnic dances and the more traditional fox trot and waltz.

The bride and groom traditionally have the first dance at the reception. The bride then customarily dances with her father while the groom dances with his mother-in-law. If any of your parents are divorced and have remarried, you may prefer to forgo the tradition of dancing with parents, and simply open the floor to guests after the newlywed dance (thus avoiding the choice between natural and step-parents). At a large wedding with a long receiving line, guests can begin dancing without you. Later on, the band leader can clear the floor for your first dance as husband and wife either before or after the first course has been cleared.

THE FIRST DANCE

Brides and grooms are choosing:

"As Time Goes By," by Hupfeld

"I'll Always Love You," sung by Taylor Dane

"(I've Had) The Time of My Life,"
sung by Bill Medley, Jennifer Warnes

"Just You and I," sung by Melissa Manchester

"Saving All My Love for You,"
sung by Whitney Houston

"Sweet Love," sung by Anita Baker

Theme from *Ice Castles,*
"Through the Eyes of Love,"
sung by Melissa Manchester

"Truly," sung by Lionel Richie

"You Are the Sunshine of My Life,"
sung by Stevie Wonder

Processional

Although the bride usually still enters the traditional way—on her father's arm—she may prefer to
stretch the rules and walk in with both her mother
and father (a custom at Jewish ceremonies). She
might want her groom and his parents to join the
processional too. Even grandparents can participate.
One bride brought the whole family together:
grandmothers and grandfathers entered first, followed by the best man (and ushers, optional), the
groom, the bride's and groom's parents, with the
maid of honor and bridesmaids, and the bride immediately behind them. When "less is more," the
bride might follow her bridesmaids down the aisle
alone, or enter arm in arm with her fiancé. When
the ceremony takes place as part of a Mass, the bride
and groom sometimes sit together at the front of the
sanctuary, and then take their places before the con-
gregation at the proper time.

If this is your second marriage and either one of

you has children from the previous marriage, ask the children to be in the processional with you. They might walk in ahead of you as you enter together. Including the children makes them feel that you are already a family, announcing your love for one another at this joint celebration.

Cake

Cakes and weddings go together like brides and grooms. The traditional cake is tiered and all white, but today it can make a highly personal statement in any flavor, color, or shape. The topper no longer need be the traditional bride and groom figurines but instead can match your wedding theme. Let your personality shine through. Sift through a few of the real-life stories and creative ideas below to see which appeal to you:

• Sarah Ferguson, whose wedding to Prince Andrew was imbued with tradition and regulated by age-old form and custom, made an individual and creative statement with her cake. Images of her favorite things—a polo player, the mythical horse Pegasus, Buckingham Palace, and her own hometown—were iced onto the five-tier fruitcake. On the top of the cake, the duchess's and duke's initials were romantically entwined.

• One petite bride, who married a six-foot-eight man, designed ''realistic'' clay figures that reflected the couple's actual height difference.

• Toppers can reflect how you met or what you do—a pair of dinosaurs, for example, if you first met at the American Museum of Natural History; whales if your first vacation together was a whale-watching trip in Maui; a miniature policeman and ballerina to reflect your respective careers or hobbies.

• A couple who met on the beach topped their cake with seashells.

• Couples who share special interests top cakes with tiny scuba divers, skiers, elephants, bears, porcelain pigs, horses, or dogs.

• Toppers can reflect where you're headed: little straw dolls for the couple en route to Mexico, hula dancers as a precursor to a Hawaiian honeymoon.

• A topper can be a custom-made work of art, made from hand-blown glass, to treasure as a keepsake.

• Your great-grandparents' topper gives your cake a sense of continuity, family history, and tradition.

• Fresh flowers remain a popular addition to the wedding cake, especially at garden or country theme weddings.

• A cake can also celebrate your background. A Scottish couple had a two-tiered wedding fruitcake, made one year in advance of their wedding to mark the Scottish one-year engagement custom. One tier is eaten at the wedding, the second saved for the birth of the first child.

• Those who relish the idea of an iced, white wedding cake topped with bride and groom will want to add the tradition of a groom's cake, made in imaginative shapes such as a champagne bottle, a duplicate of your wedding invitation, or a top hat. One couple, who celebrated a *Gone with the Wind* wedding at a southern mansion, had a groom's cake that looked like the best-selling book. His cake can be his favorite: chocolate, banana, or spice, and it is cut and served along with the bride's. Often, slices are prepacked for guests to take home as favors. (Some couples serve the groom's cake at the rehearsal dinner.)

The bride's cake is cut just before dessert at a luncheon or dinner reception. At a tea or cocktail reception, the cake can be cut after an hour or so of hors d'oeuvres. The groom places his hand over the bride's and together they cut the cake, using a ribbon-tied silver cake knife. This may be a knife that you have purchased for the occasion, a family heirloom, or one that belongs to the caterer. One father of the groom, who attended his son's wedding in a full evening dress Scottish kilt, lent the couple his ceremonial dagger (called a dirk) to cut the cake. Another pair made the first cut with a fire ax to honor the groom's occupation. At military weddings, the cake is traditionally cut with a saber or sword. The bride and groom usually feed each other the first slice. To include the families, why not personally serve both sets of parents before the cake is taken away by the caterer's staff to be cut for the guests?

Flowers

The traditional all-white bouquet is still the most popular but is no longer an absolute must. One bride carried a bouquet of thirty-six scarlet roses to match her red wedding dress. Another wore white and carried an armful of brilliantly variegated French tulips. The couple who chose a beach theme for their wedding carried it through by having the bridesmaids hold large seashells filled with flowers and adorned with ribbons. Their centerpieces were fashioned of open ceramic clam shells holding candles and dried seaweed. A couple who wanted an international theme placed a small white bud vase on each table containing an American flag (for the bride), an Australian flag (for the groom), and a single red rosebud. Flowers are an expression of your style and there are endless possibilities. Flowers might echo the season—at a December wedding, for example, a snow-white fur muff could be topped with a single white orchid. Or they might reflect your patriotism or roots. In Alaska, many brides include forget-me-nots, the state's flower, in bouquets: it adds "something blue" and symbolizes true love. One couple celebrated their different home states by adding Texas bluebonnets for her and the New Mexico state flower, a pale yellow yucca, for him, to the floral arrangements.

Brides who don't want to toss their actual bouquet after the reception are now asking florists to make a smaller duplicate, sometimes in high-quality silk. Others throw a similar bouquet of dried or silk flowers. Large bouquets that are designed to break apart allow the bride to throw a token and keep the rest as a memento. A bride might also choose flowers to wear for the reception, both on her wrist or in her hair.

The Receiving Line

No matter how untraditional the wedding, the receiving line is a custom well worth keeping. The receiving line not only ensures that every guest can speak with you and your groom, as well as the wedding party, but it also gives everyone a chance to share their feelings after an emotionally moving wedding service. Here are some dos and don'ts to keep in mind to make it work more efficiently:

• DO form a receiving line during the first half hour of the reception, allowing guests to share their best wishes and enabling you to greet each of them.

• DON'T let guests go thirsty and hungry during this time. Drinks and hors d'oeuvres should be served as guests wait to go through the receiving line. Set up a few chairs along the line, so elderly guests can rest.

• DO have the bride's mother stand at the head of the reception line to greet guests if she is the hostess of the party. Next to her is the groom's mother, followed by the bride, the groom, the maid of honor and bridesmaids, and the ushers (optional). If fathers wish to join the receiving line, they should each stand to the left of their wives. Many brides today prefer a shorter line, which does not include fathers, bridesmaids, or ushers—a thoughtful idea for large weddings.

• DON'T increase family tension where stepmothers and stepfathers are concerned. You are the best judge of your family situation and how it should be handled, but generally, it is best not to have a divorced mother and father stand together in a receiving line.

• DO ask a grandmother, aunt, or sister to stand with you and your father if you have no mother or stepmother. If the bride and groom are hosting their own reception, as many couples do today, it is appropriate for them to stand at the head of the line.

• DON'T forget to record the event. You might want to place a guest book or address book at the end of the receiving line and ask guests to sign it— a lovely keepsake.

Frequently, brides and grooms find themselves at a second reception given for them in another city, several days after the first (a Progressive Wedding). It is an excellent idea to form a receiving line, enabling guests to meet you and to thank their hosts.

At a Long Weekend Wedding, it isn't necessary

to form a receiving line at every party you attend. A line at the wedding reception is all that is needed; just be sure to get around to see everyone at other weekend events.

Seating Arrangements

The bridal party customarily sits together at the same table, sometimes elevated on a dais so the guests can see them. Bride and groom sit in the center with alternating bridesmaids and ushers on either side, starting with the maid of honor and the best man. At a separate parents' table, the couple's parents sit with the officiant. You may prefer, however, to have two separate tables, one for the bride's parents and one for the groom's. Divorced parents should not be seated at the same table. Let each host a table with his or her family and friends.

Table numbers or cards at the entrance to the reception let guests know where to sit. These table cards can easily be personalized to fit in with the theme of your wedding. Here are some ideas that may appeal to you:

• One bride placed a different centerpiece at each table and then assigned guests to "Rose" or "Daisy" tables, instead of to numbered tables.

• An athletic pair named tables after favorite sports.

• Couples have also used names of cities where they have traveled together.

• One couple named tables after famous horse tracks and races. The seating chart was designed in the shape of a racetrack and place cards were made from old pari-mutuel tickets.

• A sentimental bride used traditional numbered tables and place cards but asked all the guests to sign them with a personal note. At the end of the reception, she collected and kept them as keepsakes.

Toasts

The celebration and fun of the reception are enhanced when the bridal party toasts the day. After the first dance, the best man traditionally proposes the first toast to the bride and groom. The groom may then respond with a toast of thanks to his best man and to his in-laws, parents, and bride. The bride may toast her groom, in-laws, and parents. To add a personal and memorable touch, why not:

• incorporate the French custom of toasting each other from a silver *coupe de mariage,* a two-handled wedding goblet engraved with your initials

• include a professional toastmaster in the reception plans (Toastmasters in England wear special uniforms, make toasts to the couple, and introduce other toasters.)

• hire a comedian to tell funny stories

• have a relative with a reputation for humor act as emcee

• allow yourselves to be "roasted" (gently) by family and friends

• ask the best man to arrange a short skit or amusing song in lieu of a toast

Leaving the Reception

After the cake has been cut, use your imagination to make a wild and wonderful getaway that matches your wedding style or says something personal about you. At a Honeymoon Wedding, a couple motored off in a banner-bedecked boat for a honeymoon on the opposite shore of the same island. Another pair rode off in a fire engine from the groom's own firehouse.

Consider the following exits, which have all been used by readers of *BRIDE'S*; then add your own ideas to the list:

• by helicopter
• in a taxicab
• by airplane
• on a sailboat
• by horse and sleigh at a winter wedding
• by gondola
• astride a horse
• in a horse-drawn carriage
• atop a hay cart
• by antique car
• on a bicycle built for two
• in a hot-air balloon

- by mobile home
- via cable car

Since the bride and groom are traditionally the first to leave, guests may feel obligated to stay until they do so. But many wedding couples today stay right up to the very end. It would be thoughtful to announce in a toast that you're having such a good time, you've decided to stay with your family and friends to continue the party. This will allow guests to feel free to leave anytime after the cake-cutting ceremony is over. If you prefer to leave when there is still a party in full swing, however, you'll have a large audience to wave you off.

Do make the effort to see that guests will be able to get from the ceremony to the reception site, and back to their hotels again. If many guests are from out of town, be considerate of their needs and, if at all possible, plan a way for them to get from site to site. One couple transported everyone from the ceremony to their reception in a double-decker bus decorated with streamers, balloons, and signs. Another put everyone on a riverboat. A San Francisco bride hired a cable car. At a country theme wedding, everyone simply walked, as a group, through the center of the small village from church to reception site.

Wedding Gifts

You will probably receive wedding gifts from all the people who attend your reception and often from those who were invited but could not attend. Most presents arrive within a month of the wedding, but tradition allows a year to send them. Open gifts in private, not in front of other guests. Have your mother or a close friend help you record who gave which gift, so that you will be able to thank the givers as quickly as possible after you have received the items. Here are some dos and don'ts to help you through the new etiquette of gift giving at new-style weddings:

- DO register at a store to help ensure that gifts will reflect your taste and needs. The registry is a boon to gift givers who may not otherwise know what to get you.

• DON'T be limited in your choices. Many couples today are registering at department and specialty stores that reflect their interests. Include a boating shop, camping store, art gallery, hardware emporium, wine store.

• DO keep in mind that guests may come from all over the country. Register in a number of different cities: for china in New York, where you live; for linens in Baltimore, where your parents live; and for kitchen appliances in Phoenix, where his folks are from. If you live in a large city, register at a department store that has branches in many cities across the country.

• DON'T encourage guests to bring gifts to the wedding. Request that guests mail all gifts to your home or your parents' home either *before* or *after* the wedding. You will certainly not want guests to bring gifts to the site of a Honeymoon Wedding; carting wedding gifts around on your honeymoon will be cumbersome and an invitation to theft. Encourage guests arriving for the weekend with gifts in hand to drop the gifts off at your house before the round of parties begins. Presents left at the reception site or other party sites might get lost or forgotten.

• DO involve the groom in the decision-making process at the Wedding Gift Registry. (After all, he'll live with the gifts too!) Your fiancé will enjoy opening presents with you, as well as writing thank-you notes to the givers.

• DON'T put guests in the position of having to give you gifts if you're marrying for the second or third time. Since you probably have most of the traditional household items you need, let them decide if and what they want to give. A Surprise Wedding (see Chapter Six) relieves any pressure and gives guests a chance to be creative. Some couples have asked that, instead of the traditional wedding gift, guests donate to a specified charity in the couple's names. One couple asked that guests donate canned goods to the less fortunate through their synagogue. At a Honeymoon Wedding, you might suggest that family and friends give only small gifts (if any), in light of the expense of the trip itself. And certainly let guests know that their presence is gift enough.

• DO take advantage of the extra time at a Long Weekend Wedding and display your gifts. During the weekend, there will be opportunities for guests to stop in and see the gifts on display in your home. Place gifts all together on cloth-covered tables. Don't put a very expensive item next to an inexpensive one or two look-alikes close together. If there's a duplicate, display only one. For greater safety, increase your homeowner's insurance policy and/or ask someone to "gift-sit" when you are out of the house.

• DON'T forget to thank everyone in writing for the gifts they send. Notes should be warm, personal, and mailed as quickly as possible. Write them within two weeks for gifts that arrive before the wedding; within a month after the honeymoon for gifts received on your wedding day.

Gifts for Attendants (and Each Other)

A small gift should be given by the bride and groom to each of the attendants. Most people give the same gift to each bridesmaid and another gift to each usher. You may prefer, however, to give each a unique gift: a plant in a pretty cachepot for the usher who just moved into a bare apartment, a silver bookmark for the bridesmaid who loves to read, a monogrammed flask for the best man who is fond of good brandy.

One popular and sentimental idea: Give something that can be worn during the wedding—a necklace or earrings for the bridesmaids, cuff links or tie bars for the groomsmen. No matter what the gift, consider having it engraved. Monogramming personalizes items for each attendant: a pewter mug, blazer buttons, business card cases, or silver hair comb. If your wedding has a special theme, you might have the attendants' gifts reflect it—tiny gold pins in the shape of an anchor, yachting neckties, or brass dolphin paperweights for a nautical theme.

At a Long Weekend Wedding, gifts are given to more than just your attendants. Those who hosted parties in your honor certainly deserve a special thank you, as do the friends and neighbors who made room in their homes for your guests. Their

UNUSUAL GIFTS

China and candlesticks are traditional and basic necessities. But couples have also been given food, flowers, architectural plans, designer lamps, trips, fishing boats, theater tickets, magazine subscriptions, a year's supply of fresh fruits, video rental certificates, season tickets to sporting events, coupons good for hours of baby-sitting, use of a vacation home for a week, his and her motorcycles, gardening tools, paintings, sculptures, original music scores, a new roof for a house, hand-sewn quilts, bicycles, canoes, secret recipes, and more!

One couple was given something they really needed—a set of sails (mainsail and jib) for their boat. Another couple were surprised to find, upon returning from their honeymoon, that a toolshed had been built for them in their absence. For a different bridal couple, who had a vast book collection, friends designed a wall of bookshelves.

gifts should be different from those you give your attendants and might be something for the home— a vase, a picture frame, a glass bowl, a special plant.

Brides and grooms often give each other memorable wedding presents as well. You'll want it to be something personal and lasting. Look to some old ethnic traditions, such as a silver Dutch marriage box. This six-sided box is engraved with allegorical figures and domestic scenes. Tuck an intimate item inside the box: a tiny note, four-leaf clover, lock of your hair, or lucky coin. The groom might follow the Italian custom of giving his bride a doll as a wedding gift. (A doll dressed up for her wedding day may be the most appropriate.) Some brides are quite creative with their gifts: one gave her groom a book she wrote documenting their engagement. You might branch off from this idea and create a scrapbook of photos, movie stubs, concert tickets, love notes, and more.

Your imagination will make the gift unique. A present doesn't have to be costly or extravagant but should come from the heart. Consider framing a poem that you both love, written on parchment; making a tape of the hit tunes you've both heard over the years; or sewing a handmade quilt for your marital bed. More practical gifts are appropriate too—a camera for the honeymoon, a CD for the groom who loves music, headphones to avoid disagreements if his taste in music drives you crazy, a small TV so she can watch old movies in one room while he watches his football games in another room.

3.
The Long Weekend Wedding

Friends are flying in from Denmark, the groom's parents are driving from Delaware, and relatives are taking trains from Toledo—all to spend three days together at a fabulous family reunion and gala wedding being held in the bride's hometown of Lenox, Massachusetts. It's a Friday afternoon in early fall. The guests are looking forward to a perfect New England weekend, planned for them by the bride and groom: early-morning hikes to view the foliage; an apple orchard outing; a visit to a quaint historic inn; evenings of backgammon, cribbage, and darts in front of the fire. And, of course, plenty of New England fare—homemade blueberry muffins, roast duckling, marinated lamb chops. Both the bride and groom will share in all these events with them. This is a Long Weekend Wedding.

Moving into the 1990s, it's clear that love knows no geographical bounds. Men and women from Maine to Texas are meeting and marrying, coming together from disparate regions of the globe to form their own little corner of the world. When love takes a new direction like this, unique weddings follow. And so a new trend has been born that enables East Coast and West Coast, northern points and southern climes, to meet in the middle. The Long Weekend Wedding gives everyone a chance to convene in one place, to spend time together at a celebration and family reunion of epic proportions. When relatives and friends are scattered throughout the country, a Long Weekend Wedding often makes the most sense—and guarantees unforgettable fun. More and more couples are inviting guests to stay for several days of parties and events. With a weekend-long celebration, there's time to meet, greet, reminisce, feast, and dance. There's even a little space in between events to rest and relax.

Couples today are choosing the Long Weekend Wedding because, after having been out on their own, they want to be embraced again by family and friends. They want all the people they love to converge at once in joyous celebration of the couple's new life together. The message to guests is: We want you to be a part of our future; we want you in our lives; we want you to witness this wonderful rite of passage, our marriage.

What would *your* Long Weekend Wedding be like? Neighbors, friends, and relatives will host parties and get-togethers in your honor: a breakfast open house, a backyard barbecue, an ice-skating party, a bingo game. Of course, the central event of the weekend will still be your wedding and reception.

The parties can be extravagant or simple, urban sophisticated or rustic and outdoorsy. For example, one couple took their wedding guests into the wilderness for a weekend at the family lodge on a lake in the mountains. The rusticity was real: no electricity, just wood-burning stoves for heat and cooking. Because no roads ran to the lodge, guests had to arrive by boat, on horseback, or on foot. On the property stood a lodge, a bunkhouse, and three guest cabins—so there was plenty of room for everyone to stay together. At the reception, everyone danced to the tunes of a local fiddler. Then the bride and groom rode off into the sunset on horseback for a camping honeymoon.

A History of Long Weekend Weddings

They may be new to you, but they were de rigueur for many of our ancestors. Long celebrations come from age-old traditions of extended parties. The Greeks and Romans celebrated weddings with elaborate feasts. Medieval marriages led to lengthy, lively parties often lasting for days. Jousting tournaments, minstrels, storytellers, musical entertainment, food, and spirits were the order of the day. Friends and relations often traveled hundreds of miles to be present for the festivities.

Royalty has always known how to celebrate with pomp and circumstance. When Mary, Queen of Scots, married Henry Stewart, Lord Darnley, in 1565, the dancing and banqueting lasted for days. Lady Jane Grey, heir to the English throne, enjoyed a ten-day festival in the mid-sixteenth century. The townspeople all partook of the wedding ''beef, bread and ale.'' In the eighteenth century, one couple, members of the British aristocracy, beat her record by partying for a month! Guests feasted, hunted, fished, danced, and gambled the days away in celebration. All winnings went to the bride and groom. Americans marrying in the Colonies brought friends and relatives from distant shores to enjoy a fortnight or two of parties, shooting trips, and other events before guests sailed on the long voyage home.

Bring history to life with your own multiday celebration. You'll certainly be in good company.

Family Reactions and Concerns

When you propose the idea of a weekend wedding, you will undoubtedly meet with one of two reactions. Most people will rejoice at the idea of seeing the family and being able to enjoy one another's company in a relaxed and unhurried atmosphere. But there may be a few who won't understand your desire to create such a celebration. Those who ask ''Why all the fuss?'' probably don't realize how well thought out the celebration is. They may be worried about the expense. In reality, both families are joining forces and purses, enabling the Long Weekend Wedding to become a reality. The Long Weekend Wedding need not cost you any more than a traditional one-day wedding. Guests pay their own travel and lodging. Hosts throwing parties in your honor pick up the tab for those events. Other get-togethers you plan may be free or cost next to nothing, such as a swim at the beach or a volleyball game in the park.

Let hesitaters know some of the reasons behind the Long Weekend Wedding plan: time to spend with the people you love, an incentive for guests to come from far away, a super weekend that, in your mind, is worth the "fuss." The Long Weekend Wedding is for one and all; your wedding serves as the catalyst for a family reunion, a memorable gathering of friends and family. Everyone has the chance to get involved, to host or attend a party; guests have plenty of time to get to know one another or rekindle old friendships. Both the bride and groom can invite relatives from near and far, thus keeping the guest list fairly even on both sides. This is a time of solidarity, the joining of two families. This is the weekend for the bride to visit with her aunt Margaret, whom she hasn't seen since high school, and the time for the groom to recommune with his cousins from Austria. And better yet, Aunt Margaret and the cousins from Austria are able to meet and have the opportunity to begin a new friendship.

Guest List

Your guest list for a Long Weekend Wedding should be drawn up in much the same way as for a traditional one-day wedding. You'll have to settle on a budget for the main event first and determine how many guests you can invite. (How many will the site accommodate? How many can you afford to include?) Ask the groom to have his family make up a list of guests they want to invite too, giving them a rough idea of how many you'd like them to aim for. Since this party joins two families, and is usually hosted by both families, it's best that both families be well represented at the wedding, with no noticeable imbalance. If the groom's parents are divorced, the parent who primarily raised him should be the one to help draw up the guest list. If the divorced parents enjoy an amicable relationship, they might collaborate on the list. For a Long Weekend Wedding, feel free to invite guests from far away. They'll be more likely to attend a multiday celebration.

Friends you haven't seen in ages can also round out your list. With a three-day series of events and get-togethers, you'll have time to get reacquainted with old buddies and introduce them to new friends. To find old friends who seem to have disappeared from your life, you may have to do some investigative work. Talk to mutual friends and former teachers for leads on their whereabouts. Contact high schools or college alumni associations for recent addresses or married names. Try professional directories—available in most libraries—if your friends are now doctors or lawyers, for example. Many libraries also carry phone books for cities across the U.S. Try to track down your friends' parents; they're less likely to have moved recently.

Planning

Once you've decided on a Long Weekend Wedding and know the weekend you have in mind . . . start planning. Contact neighbors, relatives, and friends in town to find out how they can help. Who will put people up in their homes? Which relative wants to host a party in your honor? (Certainly these parties need not be costly or elaborate.) Who wants to volunteer to transport visitors to and from the airport?

Begin to sketch out a plan of how the weekend will run, deciding how many events there will be. Think about the number of people attending, and their ages and interests. Since not every event will appeal to everyone, you'll want to give guests their choice of a variety of activities. A bike ride around the lake may be great for the energetic, a tour of a museum for collectors, a quiet tea in the library of a beautiful old inn for romantics. You don't want anyone to feel left out, so balance the activities to fit many age groups and activity levels. Mix plenty of relaxed events in with the few late-night parties.

When planning, stay flexible and think of alternatives if the weekend starts to look too crowded. For example, there's no rule that says the rehearsal dinner can't take place on Thursday night instead of the night before the wedding. Such a switch could make for a more relaxed weekend.

Now write down a tentative schedule of events. Your long weekend, occurring over a holiday, might proceed like this:

Friday afternoon: Guests due to arrive at the airport. The bride's house (or a neighbor's) will be operating as a hospitality center, with coffee and drinks available. Guests are ferried in from the airport, pick up their welcome packages and maps, and head to their lodgings with neighbors or at hotels. (Welcome packages also may be left at the hotels.)

Friday night: The groom's parents host a rehearsal dinner for immediate family and wedding party. The hospitality center remains open for out-of-town guests still arriving (ask a neighbor or friend to welcome them). A friend hosts an informal sandwich buffet for guests who are not attending the rehearsal dinner.

Saturday noon: A luncheon and croquet-on-the-lawn is hosted by an aunt and uncle. Everyone is invited.

Saturday afternoon: Unlimited swimming and tennis at the club.

Saturday night: A formal 6:30 P.M. wedding in church is followed by an all-night reception.

Sunday afternoon: Guests play a softball game, and enjoy a barbecue and oompah band.

Sunday night: A piano-bar party is thrown by the bride's parents and in-laws.

Monday morning: A brunch outdoors in a relative's garden. Bride and groom say their final good-byes and head off on their honeymoon; guests leave at their leisure.

With other people pitching in to throw parties, you'll have only the wedding and one or two other events to worry about by yourself. Your main job will be to coordinate events and to get the word out to guests—by phone, newsletter, or verbal announcement—that these parties will be taking place.

Delegating

You're probably surrounded by relatives and friends eager to help out. Make use of their energy and enthusiasm so you can conserve some of your own. Think of tasks they can do for you—assign your brother to yard work in preparation for the backyard picnic; send your sister to get the wedding newsletter printed and mailed out to guests. (See sample newsletter in box, page 51.) Look at your TO DO list and ask yourself which items on this list you *must* do yourself and which someone else could do for you. Always be polite when asking for help; you certainly don't wish to offend friends or family.

Talk with all the people who have offered to give parties during the weekend. Perhaps your aunt wants to give a welcome-to-town tea for guests from afar; the maid of honor may be planning an intimate luncheon for bridesmaids only; the groom's parents want to host an elegant rehearsal dinner; your brothers and sisters say they'll put on a bride's team versus groom's team volleyball game. You may discuss preliminary ideas and even budget with them, but don't meddle in the host's role. Once you agree to let someone throw a party for you, it becomes his or hers, and you are merely an honored guest. If you're asked for your opinion and advice, go ahead and give it. (See below for fun ideas and special parties.) Share your wedding theme with those helping you. Certainly you should tell them how many guests you expect and the names of everyone on the guest list, as well as their ages and backgrounds. This will help hosts to plan. If asked, be honest about how much you think the party may cost them. A champagne and dessert gala may cost $8 to $15 a person, while a seated dinner may run $30 a head or more. Beyond this, hosts should be left in charge of making their own hosting decisions. Be sure to follow up with a gift and thank-you notes.

Special Touches and Unique Party Ideas

There'll be time for many extra touches that you wouldn't ordinarily be able to squeeze into a five-hour wedding celebration. When thinking about weekend activities, be as creative as you like. Try some of these ideas:

• Run a mini–marriage-marathon race—ending with a pool party.

• Host a clambake.

• Offer rainy-day alternatives: the showing of classic films, a bowling alley party.

• Think of creative "reunion" or "get-to-know-one-another" ideas. How about a TRIVIAL PUR-SUIT® game with special questions about the bride and groom?

• Project a custom slide show at the rehearsal dinner. Prepare a video of prewedding fun that guests may have missed—shower, engagement party, bachelorette bash. Create a film of family photos, set to music. Or use old home movies and current videos to make a "This Is Our Life" film. Include interviews with family members—funny, silly, or sentimental. Check the yellow pages for "Video Production Services" or produce a film yourself. If you need video monitors at the reception site or other party site, be sure to arrange for them in advance. Speak with your caterer and with a TV rental store.

• Assemble a photo display, including snapshots of the wedding couple from birth on up, plus photos of your guests. Show them at your reception or at one of the prewedding parties.

• Send guests off on a sightseeing tour of the city. Add the unusual: do it at night, with champagne.

• Hire an astrologer to give guests a peek into their futures at an outdoor fair.

• Announce a golf or tennis tournament with name tags and team T-shirts.

• Throw a 1950s sock hop. Rent a jukebox.

• Have a picnic in the park.

• Arrange a disco night with bus service home (so no one will drink and drive).

• Take advantage of classic photo opportunities. Snap a picture with bride and groom as each guest arrives. Post the results on a bulletin board. Let guests take them home as favors.

• Hire a cartoonist or caricature specialist to draw pictures of guests—a great party favor! Or give each guest a rose boutonniere, to symbolize true love, or a fragrant sprig of rosemary, for remembrance. Other favor ideas: One lucky bride found one hundred four-leaf clovers, which she pressed into bookmarks for each guest! Also consider personalized pencils, engraved coasters, and wine and champagne bottles with labels bearing the couple's name and wedding date.

• Host a slumber party for bridesmaids and bride only. Supply sleeping bags, sandwiches, snacks, sodas, and old 45-RPM records.

• Invite maids and moms to a beauty salon party. Arrange for a wedding morning visit to a full-service salon for manicures, pedicures, makeup, and hair styling. Make sure that the salon has been contacted in advance so space, time, and stylists have been reserved for all. Or have the stylists come to your home for a private hairdo session.

Getting the Word Out

Guests need plenty of time to plan for an ambitious weekend get-together, so send announcements and newsletters well in advance of the actual wedding invitation. Early on, family and friends should know the dates of the wedding and of surrounding events, and receive information about travel and lodging arrangements. Guests will be responsible for the cost of any travel arrangements and their hotel rooms, but you'll want to help them out by reserving rooms and researching fares.

Send guests a tentative weekend schedule to help them with their plans—mentioning, for example, that the bride and groom will be staying on after the Saturday wedding and will not leave on the honeymoon till Sunday or Monday. Make sure you also tip guests off to appropriate attire; if they know there are going to be sports activities, they'll bring jeans or shorts. An evening wedding will dictate more formal attire for wedding guests. The luncheon may necessitate a daytime dress for women, a blazer for men. Be sure, too, that guests know which parties are for them and which are closed to ''bridesmaids only'' or ''immediate family and wedding party only.'' Many brides provide alternative entertainment for guests at these times. If there are any events that will cost guests money, be sure they realize this. For example, your newsletter may state, ''Afternoon trip to the aquarium. Admission: $6 adults, $3 chil-

PENNY & RICHARD
WEDDING NEWSLETTER

GREETINGS from "WEDDING CENTRAL" in White Plains, New York. Plans for the Fourth of July weekend festivities are under way! We're giving you a preview of the schedule of events to facilitate your plans and ours.

Schedule

Friday: 7:00 P.M. REHEARSAL DINNER
(wedding party and family)
5:00 P.M. till ?? WELCOME at the Armstrongs'—buffet, refreshments, room assignments, answers to all your urgent questions. Plus: Don't miss the ongoing slide show of family and friends set up in the rec room!

Saturday: 11 A.M. BRUNCH BUFFET for everyone
(Dress: casual)
1 P.M. TENNIS TOURNAMENT at the Plains Club (sign up during the brunch; tennis whites only); puppet show for kids inside the Club House during the tournament
3 P.M. SECRET MEETING AT ELIZABETH ARDEN (bridesmaids only)
6:30 P.M. THE MAIN EVENT: PENNY AND RICHARD'S WEDDING (formal attire)

Sunday: 12:30 P.M. ALL-AMERICAN BARBECUE AND VOLLEYBALL GAME (wear something red, white, and blue!)
4 P.M. POOL PARTY at the Plains Club, light snacks available
9 P.M. ICE CREAM SUNDAE PARTY (bring your sweet tooth)
10 P.M. FOURTH OF JULY FIREWORKS and FAREWELL to Penny and Richard

Monday: 8 A.M. EARLY BIRD BREAKFAST . . . Sustenance before your departure

We hope that by now you have made your travel plans. Please fill out the enclosed card with dates, times, and flight numbers, then return the postcard to us. We will try to meet you. More on this later. We are currently locating housing and low-cost hotel rooms as well. Update to come. That's all the news for now.

Love, Penny and her "Wedding Team"

P.S. Questions? Call:
Travel: Penny's mom at (phone number)
Lodging: Uncle Bob at (phone number)
Child care: Susie at (phone number)
Other: Penny at (phone number)

dren under 12.'' This is all you need to say to alert guests to the cost of this event.

As plans progress and the time of the big weekend draws nearer, individual hosts will probably want to send out their own invitations to the weekend's special events. Or these invitations, with hosts' names on them, can be included in a welcome package given to guests upon their arrival—if they are not mailed out to everyone beforehand.

Lodging

Depending on where your wedding is being held, you might want to take over a nearby hotel or country inn, housing as many people as possible in one location, and thus getting them a special rate. Or perhaps you can find places for visitors at friends' homes. This is especially helpful for young guests who may have trouble paying for two or three nights in a hotel. Besides saving everyone money, you will provide the added benefit of togetherness. Guests get to know one another. Friends and relatives really feel a part of the weekend's festivities. Some people, however, may prefer the privacy of their own hotel room. Although it's up to you to find the hotel rooms, it's the responsibility of those staying in them to pay for the accommodations. For this reason, you should keep various budgets in mind when locating hotels. You might want to offer a choice of two locations, with two price ranges. Make sure that the lodging is convenient to most of the weekend activities, and that you have personally toured the place and seen the rooms. Know what you are recommending. Don't scatter everyone at too many different hotels, or transportation will become your biggest problem. With all of your guests staying together at one or two locations, you can easily send a bus or van to pick everyone up at once.

Transportation

Here are the dos and don'ts of guest transportation:

• DO give visitors practical travel information, with train and plane schedules and fares, names of airports and train stations, and rental car locations.

Find out about low air fares; pass this information on. In most cases, guests will pay any transportation costs themselves.

• DON'T leave guests stranded. Once your guests have made their plans, ask them to return an enclosed card listing their names, phone number, date, flight number, or train arrival and departure times. This will help you to arrange transportation to and from the airport or train station. Perhaps a large group of people is landing at roughly the same time. Why not send a van or bus, decorated with a welcome sign, to pick them all up at once? If you can't provide the transportation yourself, send guests information about taxis, buses, and limousine services running from the airport.

• DO suggest that guests reserve early for the best fares and most convenient flights.

• DON'T overlook the possibility of complimentary transportation. If guests are all staying at a resort or hotel, there may be free bus service provided by the hotel from the airport.

• DO consider how everyone will get from event to event. Make bus, van, or car-pool arrangements.

• DON'T underestimate old-fashioned foot power. Many places may be within walking distance.

• DO give everyone a map with all activity locations clearly marked on it—to help guests get around on their own. Assign each location a number, and then refer to it on corresponding lists of events. For example, ''Beach party at the Whites', #7.'' The guest would then be able to find location #7 on his map.

Guest Considerations

Always think of guests' comfort and plan ahead for their needs to ensure that all will enjoy themselves once they arrive. You'll want guests to know just how much you appreciate the effort they've made in coming to your Long Weekend Wedding. Here are some of the best ways to make guests feel pampered:

1. Make sure all those invited know in advance about every weekend event. Enclose a list of parties and activities with the invitation.

2. Keep everyone posted on changes/additions by sending newsletters.

3. Give crucial phone numbers where a guest could call for more information.

4. Make sure guests know about the seasonal climate in your town as well as the style of each event during the weekend. This will help them to plan and pack wisely for their trip.

5. Upon arrival, add welcoming touches, such as:
- transportation from the airport or train station
- a folder of information—including maps, a schedule of events, and local tour information on interesting or historical sites
- a list of invitees with information on who's staying where so guests can contact one another
- additional weekend information, such as museum hours, bicycle rental fees, names of reputable baby-sitting agencies, lists of movie theaters, synagogues and churches of various denominations, and nearby hospitals
- "welcome" packages to be left in hotel rooms or at the homes where guests are staying with friends (Include a comb, travel toothbrush, a bag of peanuts, bottle of champagne, plastic fluted glasses, antacid, aspirin.) Use your imagination! Some brides arrange for deliveries of homemade cookies, or they send flowers or fruit baskets. For extra fun: Add an item that ties into the weekend events—a baseball cap for the softball game, a bright yellow shovel or suntan lotion for the beach, a FRIS-BEE® for the park picnic, a bandana for the barbecue. Contact the local Convention and Visitors Bureau for free maps, guides, or pamphlets advertising local attractions; tuck these into the packages as well.

Guests with Special Needs

If any of your guests have special dietary restrictions or mobility problems, prepare for these in advance. Call and ask them what their needs are. If you have a friend or relative with a physical disability, make sure ceremony and reception site are accessible to and comfortable for him or her. If a guest is blind, call ahead of time to explain the layout of the church or synagogue. For wheelchairs, look for ramps that start at street level. The hotel you suggest should be equipped with wide corridors and doorways as well as elevators (that quaint little inn with the winding staircase and narrow passageways would be far from ideal). Reserve parking spaces for the disabled in front of all event locations. Offer rides to and from sites if the disabled person doesn't drive or would have trouble getting on buses. Invite your disabled guest to bring a friend along—if they wish. Ask about any required special menus—diabetic, salt restricted, kosher, etc. At the reception, seat guests who are deaf near the band so they can feel the music's vibrations. You might also want to have a sign language interpreter at the wedding or reception. Guests with special needs won't forget these kindnesses.

Small Children and Teens

If you've invited the under-eighteen set to your Long Weekend Wedding, make some special preparations for them. Interesting entertainment and favorite foods will go a long way toward ensuring happy participants. At a cocktail hour, for example, make sure the bartender will be ready with alcohol-free piña coladas, Shirley Temples, and fruit shakes. Better still, set up a separate table with favorite drinks for kids. Seat young children at their own table with a baby-sitter hired for the occasion. If you think some guests will prefer to leave their young children at the hotel, give them phone numbers of baby-sitters in the area. Or you may be able to set up an impromptu day-care situation where a number of babies and children can be left with several experienced supervisors.

At parties during the weekend, keep short attention spans in mind. Grown-up conversation can seem dull, causing kids to act wilder than usual. Counteract this natural reaction with entertainment—a magician, storyteller, or puppeteer in one room of the house—while adult luncheon chatter continues in another. By planning for children, you'll not only please them but their grateful parents as well. Teens might enjoy a separate get-together—such as a pizza party, coed softball game, tickets to a local college basketball game, or a popcorn and video party (you rent an appropriate movie). If you know very little about children, you might delegate the responsibilities of overseeing these plans to a friend, sibling, or neighbor with small children or teens of her own. She'll probably have the best ideas for activities.

Food

There'll be plenty of wining and dining, snacking and feasting going on during the weekend wedding. Keep these food tips handy as you make final plans:

• Choose foods for weekend activities that complement your wedding day fare. For example, if you will be serving roast beef at your wedding reception, you don't want to offer it at the rehearsal dinner. The point is not to have the same foods at each party, even if they are presented differently. Chicken crepes followed by barbecued chicken, for example, are still chicken.

• Vary the style and type of foods you serve during the weekend. Light picnic fare at one event should be followed by hearty meats at another, colorful cold pastas at a third. Mix informal ''grazing'' at buffet tables on some nights with seated dinners on other nights.

• Intersperse a few light-weight meals or low-calorie dishes with every meal. Many people are watching their weight these days—so, in fairness to them, offer foods that even dieters can enjoy, guilt free. Don't serve heavy sauces and rich meals on all three days.

• Avoid having only snacks at every party. Not serving a meal at one or two events is fine, but a steady fare of snack foods means guests will go hungry!

• Prepare foods that are ideal for crowds: lasagna, chili, large salads, a steamship round of beef, paella, macaroni and cheese, chicken cacciatore, roast ham, casseroles, stews, and soups.

• Freeze ahead to avoid the last-minute rush of

food preparation. You can freeze stews, soups, casseroles, lasagna, brownies, cookies.

• Include seasonal fare when appropriate: Christmas cookies in December, apple bread and cider on a fall weekend in New England, fresh fruits in the California summer sunshine.

• Give guests a taste of your region's best: Philadelphia cheese steaks, Maine lobsters, San Francisco sourdough bread, New England clam chowder, Tennessee black-eyed peas with all the fixings.

• Outdoor picnics and barbecues are a favorite at Long Weekend Weddings, but they can be disasters if you don't protect against food poisoning and other "natural" annoyances—such as ants and flying pests. Do not leave foods out in the hot sun all day. Bring coolers to keep perishable items fresh. Begin preparing the picnic site a day or two before everyone arrives, with an insecticide sprayed in the general area. Burn citronella candles at night. Keep food closed in plastic bowls with tops or wrapped in plastic wrap to protect it from flies. Unwrap foods and open the picnic buffet at the last minute, to keep everything as fresh as possible.

A Word to the Wise

In fairness to hosts and guests, the bride and groom should attend every single event of the weekend, but they needn't feel obligated to stay from beginning to end. You may prefer to put in a short appearance at prewedding parties. Stay long enough to throw out the first ball at the baseball game or to have a cup of coffee at the early-bird breakfast. Then, if you wish, you can leave to take care of other affairs or have a rest. Everyone will understand. The point is that you were there long enough to thank the hosts of the party and to greet guests. The party is, after all, being thrown in honor of you, the wedding couple.

THE SENTIMENTAL JOURNEY

The waves are lapping at the shore of the beach where you spent every summer since you were a child. As you drive up the winding road, you can see the old white house rising up on the dunes, its pillars wrapped with wedding day streamers and balloons. Sea gulls are darting and diving overhead. Your youngest nieces and nephews are playing tag on the wide front lawn. Great-aunts and uncles are seated comfortably in white lawn chairs. Gentle summer breezes promise good times—volleyball, sandcastle competitions, clambakes, swimming. This is a return to summers past, a Sentimental Journey for the wedding couple and all their guests.

A Long Weekend Wedding at a site that has special meaning to the bride and groom or their families is a Sentimental Journey into the past for everyone who attends. Perhaps the bride and groom want to return to their alma mater to marry at their college chapel and host the reception somewhere on campus. Or the couple may choose to take a Sentimental Journey back to the beaches of Cape Cod or Monterey, where both families summered while the children were growing up.

This type of wedding can be perfect for couples who would rather not marry in the bride's hometown but who still want to choose a location that holds special meaning for both of them. Think about towns that have captured your hearts, places that play host to good memories. Does the groom have a Sentimental Journey he'd like to make? If the spot you choose is far away, see the section on planning from afar (in Chapter Four).

The Sentimental Journey should be held over a weekend, giving you and your guests a chance to relive good times and enjoy the trip down memory lane. Check the section above on Long Weekend Weddings for practical planning ideas that will help you with your Sentimental Journey wedding. Consider how many people will be able to fit at your Sentimental Journey site. Is your mountain cabin big enough to accommodate more than your immediate family? If not, research nearby lodges and inns for adequate space. Your college campus might be willing to rent out empty dorm rooms for a nominal fee over the summer, enabling some of your guests to relive those college days in the very rooms they once inhabited. Try to take over one wing or one dorm so everyone's together. You might prefer to book a special hotel suite for yourself instead, away from the hubbub. You'll want to pamper yourself with every luxury a bride deserves during the wedding weekend—so that you'll look your best!

For a Sentimental Journey filled with the best memories, consider these special touches, which can be conceived and hosted by wedding attendants, friends, and relatives. Let everyone know you welcome their ideas, help, and hosting skills.

• Assemble a slide show of the past events you're celebrating now: shots from your college days if you're marrying at your old alma mater or summers on the lake if you're back at the rustic camp you attended as a child.

• Plan your wedding celebration around a reunion year for your class and add to your wedding fun by joining already-planned fêtes such as the Friday-night campus dance or Saturday-morning prayer service. An added bonus: Many of the guests you invite will be having a Sentimental Journey of their own.

• Invite friends to sing old college or camp songs; provide the words and sheet music for everyone.

• Hire the school's marching band to walk along with you, providing rollicking musical accompaniment as you, the bridal party, and your guests all walk together from the chapel to the reception site. Request a mixture of college songs and other tunes for *auld lang syne.*

• Organize a tag football game. Give everyone who plays a scarf with school colors or college T-shirt in two "team" colors.

• Plan a nostalgic visit to old childhood haunts, such as the amusement park near your summer cottage. Give everyone tickets for a ride on the roller coaster.

• Take everyone to a comedy club or theater if your Sentimental Journey takes place in the city (New York? Chicago? Los Angeles?) where you and your family lived during your high school years.

• Stage a canoe race at a Sentimental Journey to the summer camp you all attended.

• Assemble old friends to share their musical and theatrical talents with a short performance, song, or funny skit based on the memories you all share.

• Plan a midnight swim on the beach. A throwback to the good old days, this event will make all of you feel like teens again.

• Did all of the cousins gather annually at your summer mountain home for a fishing competition? Make time for an instant replay. Offer rods to one and all, and compete for the biggest trout one more time.

4.
Travel Weddings

A Travel Wedding might involve a journey for the couple, the guests, or both. At a Honeymoon Wedding, bride, groom, and guests all pack their bags and head for the surroundings that suit them best: a French château, an Amsterdam canal boat, or a Vermont ski slope. At a Progressive Wedding, only the couple travel, going from place to place and following their hearts, as they visit all those they love. During a Progressive Wedding, they'll be toasted and hosted by friends and family across the country or around the globe at a string of marriage celebrations.

THE HONEYMOON WEDDING

As soon as the wedding party and guests touch down on Bermuda, a tiny island six hundred miles off the coast of Cape Hatteras, North Carolina, they feel the warmth of gentle breezes and know the excitement of a Honeymoon Wedding. A pink and blue public bus picks them up at the airport and winds its way past small white-roofed homes and manicured lawns dotting the low hills. The delicious sight and scents of hibiscus, bougainvillaea, oleander, and morning glory fill everyone with a sense of excitement and anticipation. At the picture-perfect beach wedding two days later, the sand is pink; the waters, turquoise; and the bride, all in white. But activities don't stop with the wedding. Everyone is together for sunny days of snorkeling, fishing, and golf, and for evenings of poolside parties, fine dining, and dancing to calypso music. This is a Honeymoon Wedding for all to experience and savor.

Tying the knot in a uniquely romantic location, on a wind-swept beach or in a faraway castle, may be your idea of wedding perfection. Even if the castle or the beach of your dreams is hundreds of miles away—in Jamaica, Hawaii, or Scotland—you can easily follow your fantasy. Today, many couples are celebrating weddings that combine an ideal honeymoon location with a splendid and intimate ceremony—an attractive option for the two of you and your families. The Honeymoon Wedding is especially well suited to couples who have children from prior marriages, because it allows the two merging families to spend time together. Other couples find that a Honeymoon Wedding is one way to keep the celebration small and intimate.

The Honeymoon Wedding can, however, be whatever you want it to be: intimate and informal, or large and elaborate. The budget for this style of wedding may be generous or modest. You can keep the cost of the reception down by keeping guest lists small. Remember, most guests (if not all) will be responsible for their own airfare and hotel costs, although you or your parents may want to pay for younger siblings or elderly grandparents who might not otherwise be able to afford the trip.

The Honeymoon Wedding need not be in Paris or Hawaii. More rustic getaways are ideal for some. One couple married in a state park, had a barbecue reception, danced around the campfire, and then took off into the woods—with guests—for a group camping trip. Occasionally, the wedding is last-minute and may involve no one other than the bride and groom. One couple traveling in Japan decided to marry at a Shinto shrine near Tokyo and startled friends and relations by returning home from vacation as Mr. and Mrs.

Even Hollywood stars want to get into the act.

When Barbara Stock of the TV show "Spenser: For Hire" married film producer Bill Dunn, they tried to plan their wedding as each continued working on different coasts. In the end, they simplified their lives by heading straight to Carmel Valley, California, where they were married in a private ceremony at a historic mansion with close friends and family.

The honeymoon celebration can blend togetherness with private time. After the wedding, the bride and groom might want to bid a fond farewell to all and travel to another part of their itinerary—a different hotel, perhaps an entirely different resort area, or a neighboring island. Nautical couples might rent a boat and sail off for the honeymoon—as guests wave good-bye from the beach. While the bride is still close enough to the shore or the dock, she tosses her bouquet from the bow. Family and friends are welcome to stay behind to continue their vacations. This way, the couple experience a honeymoon alone together—after the fun of vacationing and wedding in a group setting.

Choosing a Location

You'll be choosing a Honeymoon Wedding location in much the same way that you would choose a honeymoon destination. Some couples return to a favorite vacation spot, while others choose an island—from books or pamphlets—that fulfills their fantasy, even though they've never been there before. Here's the best way to conduct your search:

• Research locations in libraries, travel magazines, and guide books.

• Contact tourist boards and travel agents for advice.

• Ask friends who have firsthand knowledge about some of the places you're considering. Get their observations and recommendations.

• Read BRIDE'S Honeymoon Travel Guide for ideas and tips on the world's most romantic locations and most sensuous suites. The book gives first-rate descriptions and provides an overview of many of the places you may be considering.

• Find out about typical weather in various locations during the season you plan to visit. Perhaps you'll decide Bermuda is too cold in December or Madrid is too hot in August.

• Talk about the kind of place that matches your dreams. Are you drawn to a Mexican village or a guest ranch in Montana? The Virgin Islands or Venice?

• Look at photos, study maps, or write for hotel brochures to help you make an informed decision.

• Think of a location that already has some special meaning for you—perhaps a place discovered on a previous vacation or the resort where one of you spent summers as a child. One couple chose a Greek island because it was the site of their first trip together. For them it was a sentimental journey back to a romantic spot they first shared as a couple. They already knew a few people from their last visit, including a travel agent and a resort manager, who were able to help them plan and organize their once-in-a-lifetime wedding. After the wedding, the couple sailed on to explore a new group of Greek islands.

• Before your hearts are set on a location, look into the rules and residency requirements for marrying there. Some islands, like Aruba and Bonaire, make it virtually impossible for American or other foreigners to marry there. Each and every state and country has different laws and regulations; France requires a thirty-day residency prior to a wedding. Some are longer than others. For example, in Bermuda, a Notice of Intended Marriage—published in a newspaper—must be filed two to three weeks before the wedding, but the couple need not be in Bermuda during this time.

• Once you've chosen a place, you'll want to narrow down the area in which you'd like to stay. If beaches are of maximum importance, find the resort that has the best beachfront property. If the view is more important, investigate a mountaintop inn overlooking the bay.

Preparing for the Trip

As soon as you decide on your destination, take steps to find out about the specific, current marriage laws. Assume nothing. Follow these steps.

1. Contact the consulate or tourist board for preliminary information if you're planning a foreign wedding. Write to the American Embassy in the country where you plan to marry. If marrying within the U.S., call the marriage license bureau in the city or state in which you plan to marry.

2. Allow yourselves plenty of time to comply with the rules and regulations. The marriage application period can be lengthy; you may need at least three months to go through channels. Overseas mail can cause further delays.

3. Once you know what documents are required, begin compiling the proper papers. The government (or marriage license bureau) will want records such as passports; proof of birth (notarized birth certificates, not photocopies); proof of citizenship; parental consent for minors; blood tests; proof of divorce from, or death certificate for, a former spouse if either of you was married before; and/or a letter from your clergy member. Even if some of these items are not specifically mentioned, carry them with you, just in case. (It's a long way home for a forgotten certificate.) Some unexpected residency requirements may exist, as well. France, for instance, asks that one of you live there for 40 days before marrying. In most non–English-speaking countries, every document must be translated, often with official seals attached. Most countries require an affidavit stating that neither person is currently married and that the couple are not related to each other. This would usually be obtained at the American Embassy in the foreign country.

4. Couples determined to marry abroad but brought to a halt by complicated regulations might want to consider legally marrying in a quiet ceremony at home, then traveling to a foreign destination for a festive reaffirmation ceremony and reception. Happily, destinations like Hawaii, Puerto Rico, Jamaica, and the U.S. Virgin Islands are accus-

tomed to visitors flocking to their shores to say "I do," and make it very easy for couples to do so. But some states and countries are sticklers for detail, have tight controls, or are awash in red tape: they may demand the document translations mentioned above, or require other items that are difficult for you to produce.

5. Check with the U.S. government. Will you have to register your marriage with a U.S. Embassy if you marry abroad? Check with the State Department as well. Do your home state and surrounding states legally recognize out-of-state/out-of-country marriages?

The Guest List

Any number of people can join you at your Honeymoon Wedding: only a few close friends or close family, just yourselves, or a planeload of people. Although many friends and relatives may not be able to join you due to the extra time and expense involved in the trip, all will appreciate the fact that you thought of them with an invitation. Others may surprise you. Your young, single, and mobile friends may jump at the chance to "jet set" off to a tropical location for a few days of spirited wedding festivities. Distant as well as close relatives may find this the perfect way to combine the vacation they need with the small family reunion they've been meaning to arrange. If there is someone you simply *won't* get married without, check with them before your plans progress too far. If that person can't come, change the date or location of the wedding.

Most guests will pay for their own trips—but if you or your parents can afford it, you might finance the travel arrangements of special family members. Let guests know that their presence is a great wedding gift—they needn't buy you anything else.

Keep guests' budgets in mind when choosing resort or hotel accommodations. You may be able to arrange less expensive group rates with hotels. Although it's ideal to have everyone stay at the same place, you might want to suggest a choice of hotels with a variety of budgets. Or book rooms at various rates. Ocean-view rooms will cost more than pool-view. Pool-view often costs more than garden-view. Ask single friends if they'd prefer a roommate—so that room charges can be split. Otherwise, you can book a separate room for each single person.

Family Concerns

Although most people will agree that a Honeymoon Wedding sounds fabulous, you may have a few family members or friends who will be shocked to hear of your plans to marry abroad or far from home. If much of the concern is coming from your own parents or future in-laws, you'll have to settle their fears and concerns before you proceed. Try to determine what their reservations are. Is your future father-in-law worried about your plans to marry abroad because he's afraid of the food, politics, language? Perhaps you could change course for an American destination like Hawaii. Is your mother fretting about the loss of the big hometown wedding of *her* dreams? Worrying that people who have known you for years won't be able to see you get married? If there's still room in the budget, suggest that she throw a second reception for you and your groom at home after the honeymoon. She'll be able to invite as many friends as she wishes. You could even wear your wedding dress again to give her celebration authenticity.

Planning a Wedding from Afar

Long-distance planning needn't be overly complicated or time-consuming if you do it right. Here are some basic tips to follow:

1. Long before your arrival, you'll want to contact a specialist at your destination who will be able to mastermind your celebration. Ask your hotel for the name of a wedding consultant who can contact an officiant, and arrange flowers and music, food and beverages, and much more at your reception site. You'll be happy to hear that many hotels have their own wedding consultants and caterers on staff, and are adept at helping couples arrange marriage parties. Some hotels even have complete wedding packages available. Check into their packages; find out exactly what they cost and what they include.

2. Contact tourist boards and travel agents for help with local customs (Is there a special wedding flower? A wedding song?) and hotel recommendations.

3. Consider the possibility of making a prewedding trip to the site to arrange important details.

4. Think about writing up and sending out a "Guide to Our Wedding" for the guests who respond "yes" to your invitations. The guide could include information on modes of travel, even fares to and from your wedding/honeymoon location. Tuck in a brochure describing attractions guests can enjoy if they choose to stay on for a short holiday after the nuptials. A thoughtful extra: A map of the area will allow guests to plan their routes, get to know names of streets and towns in advance.

5. Explain all your crucial requirements to your contact at the site. If you want flowers native to the island, a videotape of the ceremony, a particular color theme or unusual getaway, make your wishes clear early on. You don't want a lack of good communication to jeopardize the smooth flow of your day.

6. Budget for long-distance telephone calls. You'll probably be talking frequently with hotel personnel, caterers, ceremony officiants, and so forth. Find out when you can call at special rates, who has a fax machine, how reliable overnight mail is, etc.

7. Spell out everything you want clearly in letters, followed up with additional instructions and confirmations when necessary.

8. Have contracts for wedding services drawn up and sent to you. Read the fine print carefully. Secure all reservations with deposits.

9. Arrange to arrive a few days before guests so you can finalize paperwork, settle last-minute questions, meet with your officiant, and check on flowers, the caterer, and the site. If you cannot arrive early, meet with your contact immediately after checking in to make sure everything is in order.

10. Give an accurate head count to the caterer as soon as you know how many people will be attending the party.

Wedding Attire

Many styles and fabrics pack beautifully and look at home at a Honeymoon Wedding location. Consider lace, satin, cotton, chiffon, cotton voile, silk crepe. Unless you want to spend time ironing, avoid linen and silk taffeta, which wrinkle easily, and polyester, which is hot when worn in the sun. Climate and ambience dictate the look. To marry atop a mountain or on the beach, something romantic yet indestructible is the goal. A hot tropic sun means a formal high neck and long sleeves are out of the question—you'll need clothes that are breezy, looser, lighter. Today's filmy, airy dresses made in layers of white chiffon or organza are a feminine—and practical—choice.

Be sure to ask the bridal store where you buy your dress to pack it carefully in its own box. Check the box through as fragile luggage rather than trying to pack it in your suitcase. Or if you feel that such a precious and necessary item might be at risk in the baggage compartment, bring the box on board with you. A third alternative: Place the dress in a garment bag and carry it over your arm, then give it to the flight attendant to hang. If there are any minor wrinkles on arrival, use a hand steamer to bring the dress back to life.

Another idea to keep in mind: Why not borrow from the fashion and style popular in your chosen location? Start with a traditional white bridal gown for the wedding and change into native attire for the reception—a kimono in Japan, *tapa* skirts in Fiji, a white *holoku* gown in Hawaii. One bride wore a *holoku* gown while her groom dressed in all white with red accents—a custom from the days of monarchy in Hawaii. This same couple wore open-ended wedding leis (garlands) of maile leaves at their beach ceremony.

Foreign Flavor

You've come a long way to be in an interesting locale, so take advantage of local customs, foods, music, style, and language, where appropriate, for a meaningful and memorable celebration. In Hawaii, order a luau of roast pig, poi, and fresh island fish.

DESTINATION DILEMMAS

Common snags can occur as you set out on your Honeymoon Wedding trip. Take precautions. Remember—your plane tickets are like cash. If you lose them, anyone who finds them can use them. Report your loss immediately to the travel agent or airline.

If you manage to arrive at your destination but your luggage does not, file a loss report with the airline before you leave the airport. Keep your claim checks. After twenty-four hours, most airlines will reimburse you for up to fifty percent of its luggage coverage—if you have receipts—so you can buy new clothes. If your wedding dress was in the lost luggage, explain this particular situation to the airline personnel. They may be more sympathetic and may reimburse you for your loss sooner (especially if the wedding is the next day).

Upon arrival at the hotel, if you or your guests have any troubles (twin beds when a double was reserved, or a missing reservation), calmly speak with the office manager. Explain the problem and your unique situation, and the hotel will usually find a way to satisfactorily remedy the situation.

Invite a trio of ukulele players or arrange for fire dancers as entertainment. Decorate with fragrant pikake flowers. One couple married on an ocean cliff in Maui and had a native singer serenade them with the "Hawaiian Wedding Song." In Bermuda, arrange for a classic English tea at your afternoon reception, with elegant finger foods served on the best china or silver. Use the colors of Bermuda—warm pastels—when choosing floral arrangements and tableware. A straw boater for the groom and a chiffon scarf for the bride can complete the breezy ease of the day. Bride and groom can escape via one of Bermuda's popular methods of transportation: horse and carriage, or motorscooter. Honeymoon Weddings give you the freedom to be you. One bride waited until the day after her wedding to throw her bouquet—on the beach, while dressed in only a bathing suit.

Favors and Keepsakes

You'll want to take back all the wonderful memories, as will your guests. Besides making photos, use your imagination to think up creative favors for everyone who attends:

• Present your parents with a painting or watercolor done by a local artist.

• Give guests tapes of local music.

• Surprise everyone with cookbooks specializing in recipes of the region.

• One couple gave away freesia bulbs with tags attached that read "When these bloom, be reminded of our love." If your Honeymoon Wedding takes place in Holland, tulip bulbs would be ideal favors or keepsakes.

• If everyone flies to the honeymoon site, individual luggage tags that read "On Our Way to Julie and Bob's Wedding, May 17, 1990" would be in keeping with the spirit of the event.

• Will the wedding take place on an island cruise ship or yacht? Give each guest a colorful nylon boat flag with initials and date to remember the day.

• For yourselves, an aerial photo of the wedding site, a collection of shells from secluded beaches, or a stash of matchbooks saved from romantic cafés may be among the nicest keepsakes.

• Put together a postcard diary as a memento. Collect postcards from favorite spots. (You might even mail them home to yourself.) Upon returning home, slip them into the clear plastic pages of a binder.

• Find out about the best shopping "buys" and consider purchasing an item the country is known for: English bone china in Bermuda, hand-painted clay pottery in Spain, fine wines in France, embroidered sweaters in Portugal, coral jewelry in the Caribbean, or fancy teas in England.

THE PROGRESSIVE WEDDING

The groom's relatives are in Phoenix, the bride's are in Boston, and the couple's joint friends live in Chicago. What can be done? The Progressive Wedding! The couple marries at the bride's home in Boston, then travels on to Chicago, where friends host a festive all-night reception at an old haunt. This is followed by a trip to Phoenix for a formal seated dinner thrown by the groom's parents and attended by all the members of his family.

When everyone cannot travel to one location to celebrate a wedding, the bride and groom can travel to them. That's the definition of a Progressive Wedding. How does it work? Quite simply, the couple visits family and friends across the country, stopping at predetermined spots for feasts and fêtes in their honor. This type of celebration works especially well for couples who have large groups of family and friends in many different locations across the country, or for a bride or groom with divorced parents who don't want to attend the same event.

The parties thrown during the course of a Progressive Wedding may be just as formal as the first wedding reception, complete with printed invitations, wedding cake, champagne, and receiving line. They may be informal, low-key get-togethers, or anything in between. A formal party might be arranged by the groom's parents or grandparents, allowing everyone in his hometown to see him grown and married, and to meet his new bride. Some brides choose to wear their wedding gown again at formal parties following the actual ceremony. Most others choose a dressy cocktail dress instead. Wedding gifts are not a necessity, but they may be sent by close friends and relatives. The party is really for well-wishers.

Invitations

An invitation for a formal party that takes place after the wedding has occurred might look like this:

Mr. and Mrs. Thomas Disk
request the pleasure of your company

at a reception in honour of
Mr. and Mrs. John Disk
Sunday, the twenty-first of September
at six o'clock
Cool Springs Country Club
Durham, North Carolina

R.s.v.p.
123 Mockingbird Road
Durham, North Carolina 27701

The progressive parties following your wedding needn't be formal, however. They may simply be large cocktail parties or buffets hosted by you or by your relatives or friends. If you are hosting your own party and wish to send out printed invitations, here is a sample:

Alice Winters and John Disk
request the pleasure of your company
Saturday, the tenth of October
at five o'clock
Twin Oaks Inn
Middlebury, Vermont

R.s.v.p.
22 Shady Lane
Middlebury, Vermont 05753

On the other hand, you may wish to include two or more celebrations on one invitation so all guests know what your plans are. A second benefit: You can send the same invitation to everyone. For example, a card that opens to reveal printing on both sides might read:

Mr. and Mrs. Bruce Winters
request the honour of your presence
at the marriage of their daughter
Alice Jane
to
John Disk
Saturday, the sixteenth of September
at twelve o'clock
Saint Mary's Church
Chicago, Illinois

Reception will be held
immediately after the ceremony
Windy City Hotel
Chicago, Illinois

R.s.v.p.
50 Lake Road
Northbrook, IL 60002

A second reception will be held
Saturday, the twenty-ninth of September
at two o'clock
Cool Springs Country Club
Durham, North Carolina

R.s.v.p.
Mr. and Mrs. Thomas Disk
123 Mockingbird Road
Durham, North Carolina 27701

Enclose two reply cards—one for each event—so guests will know how and where to respond.

Planning the Trip

Like any other type of wedding, the Progressive Wedding requires thoughtful planning. You'll want the whole trip to go smoothly, so follow this nine-step plan:

1. First, talk with your fiancé, his family members, and your friends. Would traveling to your wedding in another part of the country or the world be difficult for them? If so, let them know you're considering traveling to them—having a Progressive Wedding—and see what they think. If they like the idea, they'll probably offer to host some parties and get-togethers in your honor. You may decide to host a party yourselves—perhaps a cocktail hour at a favorite restaurant for all your friends in New York.

2. If the idea seems to be welcomed by everyone, start mapping out your trip. Where should you stop? Choose the cities and towns closest to the largest number of people. Can your groom's grandmother travel from her home in Atlanta to your in-laws' home in North Carolina, or should you arrange a party closer to her?

3. Decide where the actual wedding will take place and whether you will marry before or after the "progression" begins.

4. Contact a travel agent. Give the agent the names of the cities you wish to go to as well as the general dates of your trip. Have the agent help you plan the order of your trip and work out the logistics of travel. You may be able to get some special airline tickets. For example, you might buy a ticket from New York to Los Angeles and stop over in Saint Louis free of extra charge. Ask your travel agent about fares that include one layover city before your final destination. If so, great! You've just managed two cities on your list for the price of one. Adjust schedules accordingly.

5. Get back to everyone involved and tell them the exact dates of your visit. Give those who have offered to host a party in your honor plenty of time to plan and invite guests. You might want to brainstorm about parties you would enjoy, or leave it entirely up to them. Each celebration you travel to can be unique and different. Each one will obviously be imbued with the style of the people hosting and attending it. Your in-laws' country club dinner, for example, will be very different from your friends' informal barbecue. If asked, give your suggestions: "We'd love a clambake on the beach!" or "I know Bob's favorite restaurant in Philadelphia has always been Smithy's." The people giving these parties want to please you.

6. Begin to plan the parties that you will be hosting. The actual wedding will be your largest concern. Family and friends will probably be the hosts of the other parties. If you are hosting one of the parties (other than the initial wedding celebration) yourself, however, you would be wise to appoint someone in that city to make arrangements with caterers, florists, and so on for you. And you might want to arrive a few days before the festivities—to help set everything up. (See the section "Planning a Celebration from Afar" on page 79 for more information.)

7. The hosts of these parties will send out their own invitations, but they are sure to ask for—and

you can politely give—some suggestions for the guest list. In any case, you'll want to know who has been invited and who will be able to come. (Will Aunt Mary be there? Is Bob's former third-grade teacher well enough to attend?) Depending on the style of the reception, invitations may be formally printed and sent out by the hosts, or the inviting may be done informally through notes or phone calls. (See above for suggestions on printed invitation wording.)

8. If your parents or in-laws are throwing a formal second reception in your honor, suggest a receiving line to give all the guests (including those you may not know) the opportunity to meet one another.

9. Have a great time. Follow up with thank-you notes to your hosts. Bring them special gifts or keepsakes from the wedding. (See below for some ideas.)

Extras

Special touches and creative extras can work to make everyone feel a part of a Progressive Wedding. For example:

• Have pieces of your original wedding cake boxed to bring to each host on your cross-country trip.

• Serve bottles of the champagne you poured at the wedding reception, to toast each other and your hosts before the hosts toast "the newlyweds."

• New York City (the Big Apple) couples might bring a shiny red apple favor for every guest attending a second reception in the next city or state.

• A couple who marries in front of the Washington Monument in Washington, DC, might give Washington quarters—a proof set minted in your wedding year—to guests at all subsequent parties on their progressive tour.

• Souvenirs from the city where the wedding was held make meaningful favors for follow-up parties. Couples coming from Minnesota, for example, might give bags of wild rice tied with ribbon; from a wedding in the Southwest, a piece of pottery.

• Instead of simply having two receptions, some couples actually have two weddings. One couple married in the groom's hometown with 250 people in attendance (including the bride's parents) and went on a honeymoon before continuing on to the bride's hometown, where a second wedding and reception were held. The bride wore her wedding dress again (her parents had it cleaned after the first wedding) and carried the same bouquet, which was made of silk flowers. The groom rented a duplicate tuxedo. They then repeated their vows in church in front of another 250 people from the bride's side of the world.

• One couple married in Hawaii, then gave a Hawaiian theme party for friends in Chicago. Aloha banners, Hawaiian leis, a luau banquet, and a wedding cake decorated with palm trees brought the fun and excitement of a Honeymoon Wedding home to their friends in the Windy City.

• Another couple brought the Bahamas home via a videotape. They let their wedding and honeymoon run nonstop on a monitor in another room during a second reception—so guests could view the film at their leisure. People will appreciate seeing photos or a videotape of the wedding ceremony, if it has already taken place. Show friends in Maryland photos or a videotape of the reception given for you by your groom's grandmother in Tulsa.

• Video technology has progressed to the point where we can see "around the world." One couple had their wedding ceremony broadcast by satellite into the living room of the groom's parents thousands of miles away—where a festive reception was being held in their honor. For these parents and their friends, it was almost as good as being there. The bride and groom traveled on to see them in person within the next few days.

• Put together a scrapbook of your progress and show it at each event. Ask guests to add to it with drawings, comments, good wishes, small memorabilia, snapshots. Miniature versions of this special scrapbook chronicling your trip could make wonderful gifts for your families as well as hosts of any parties held in your honor.

• Any group of friends along the way could consider your wedding a reason to create an amusing cabaret show about your lives—singly and as a couple.

• Combine all the elements for one last bash. At one California wedding, which marked the end of a cross-country progression of parties, the buffet represented all the various regions the couple had visited: New Orleans Cajun specialties, a favorite of the groom; lobster (flown in fresh) from the bride's native Maine; cheesecake from their own New York City.

• For an unusual keepsake, one couple took the same white tablecloth to be signed by the guests at each party. Everyone used a water-soluble embroidery pen; later the bride traced their signatures with embroidery. (It is important to note that ink in these pens is designed to fade over time, so do the embroidery soon after your wedding—before the signatures disappear.) The tablecloth can be used at every anniversary dinner.

• A tasteful idea: Buy a cloth-covered blank book and have close relatives and friends at the wedding and subsequent parties write in their favorite recipes. You'll have a lifetime of culinary delights from both sides of the family, from Grandma's risotto to Aunt Maria's paella.

INTERNATIONAL PROGRESSIVE WEDDINGS

Progressive Weddings will take some cross-cultural couples farther than our shores, as they travel to foreign lands to share the happiness of their marriage with relatives and friends far away. One couple married in front of 500 guests at an Istanbul Art Nouveau palace, then remarried before another group, of 450 guests, in New York. Another couple married in the groom's native England to accommodate guests who couldn't travel all the way to America. They then flew to their home in Connecticut to share in a second celebration—with a slide show of the British nuptials and the bottom tier of their English wedding fruitcake.

If either the bride or the groom is a citizen of the country in which they wish to marry, wedding plans should be fairly straightforward and there should be little more to worry about than what to pack. If the couple is American but has many relatives and friends abroad, the story is different. Contact the consulate of the foreign country and begin making the necessary arrangements early on. If marriage for an American in that country seems difficult, marry in the U.S. and enjoy a second reception abroad as husband and wife with relatives or friends. One native New Yorker who married her Israeli fiancé in Tel Aviv was living there at the time and able to make all her own arrangements. A second party for the two of them back home in New York was left entirely in her mother's hands. The bride concentrated on her own wedding plans in Israel and arrived in the States relaxed and ready to be an honored guest at the next party. A bride from the Philippines married her Spanish fiancé at his family's private chapel just outside Madrid. His parents paid for and arranged all the festivities. The couple, who reside in San Francisco, then flew off on a round-the-world honeymoon lasting four months, stopping, of course, in the Philippines to visit the bride's parents, who were unable to attend the wedding. There was great excitement—because they had never met the groom before!

Not everyone wants to, or can, leave all the planning to someone else. If you're in charge of both events, including one celebration abroad, you'll probably needs lots of help from family, friends, and wedding professionals. See the following section on long-distance planning.

Planning a Celebration from Afar

If you're in one location and the wedding is taking place in another, plan ahead, delegate tasks to trusted friends and relatives, be flexible, and expect many happy surprises. One bride managed the execution of a perfect wedding from aboard a sixty-four-foot sailboat. She communicated with her parents back home in Connecticut and with party planners at the wedding and reception site in French Polynesia by short-wave radio. Why the strange circumstances? Her fiancé proposed to her as they set out from Los Angeles on a round-the-world trip aboard their own sailboat! For those of you planning from dry land:

• Rely on your parents if they're available. When you're bogged down with work and far from the wedding site, you may feel most comfortable letting them do the planning for you.

• Contact a friend or relative who is "on the scene" to be your eyes and ears. Such a person could look at a reception site for you or listen to a band play at a local hotel. It's essential that you and she have similar tastes.

• Hire a bridal consultant at the wedding location. A good one can save you time and trouble, especially when you are marrying in a distant town and are not familiar with the wedding resources available. The consultant will be responsible for arranging flowers, photographs, food, music, drinks. You will always be the decision maker, but the consultant can carry out your wishes, handle the details, advise you of his or her progress, and, in your absence, arrange the party you want. Top bridal pros know the best caterers, the finest sites, good photographers, etc. What's more, they have clout. They've worked with the vendors and shop owners before, and are able to recommend the best talent, the best value.

• If you prefer, hire a bridal consultant in your own town who has good contacts in the city where you plan to marry. Some consultants are able to handle long-distance planning because they are familiar with the city, know other consultants and caterers there, or travel there from time to time.

• Divide planning tasks among several friends or relatives, based on their expertise. Send each clips from bridal magazines. For example, ask your brother to handle transportation. Let him know that he's in charge of hiring the limousines, arranging for rides for out-of-towners, chartering a bus if needed. Ask a friend who sews to create personalized favors for guests.

Whenever one of your "foot soldiers" makes an arrangement, tell them to get it in writing. The contract should list complete price, payment schedule, the site and date of delivery, the name of the person doing the work, and any other special stipulations. For example, the photographer's contract should spell out the number of photos to be taken, how long proofs can be kept, and whether prints come in an album. List important wedding shots, plus any special needs or requests: early arrival at your home, getaway shots at the harbor. To be on the safe side, the contract should also give the name of the person who would substitute if the photographer was unable to meet his or her obligation, and what restitution would be made if the photographer didn't come or if the prints were of poor quality. Have your helpers send copies of all contracts to you.

• Clip ideas and photos from bridal magazines, and send them on to those who are planning and plotting. One bride who wanted a Spanish friend to hand-make a lace mantilla for her sent clips of the headpieces she preferred. Armed with these examples, the friend was able to create an heirloom treasure for her wedding day. If you want your sister to scout bridesmaids' dresses for you, send her advertisements and magazine photos with your favorite styles. Also send a photo of your dress with a detailed description, so she can try to match its look in the bridesmaids' dresses. Do the same for the ushers' outfits. Have your brother research prices and availability at rental stores. With men's formal-wear chains, you can choose the outfits personally at the store nearest you, then transfer that order to the stores nearest your attendants or wedding site.

• Use all the high-tech resources that are available to you. Communicate by fax, overnight mail, etc., to send sketches, drawings, and photos quickly and accurately. Ask if your bridal consultant and other vendors have fax machines.

• Visit the wedding site. If possible, make at least one or two trips to your wedding town before the actual festivities begin. You may need to see the reception area and to speak with the caterer and florist in person. Perhaps there are contract negotiations you'll want to settle yourself. Furthermore, this visit will give you a good chance to meet with your "troops" and your bridal consultant, to confirm their plans so far, to answer their questions, and to reiterate your dreams.

5.
Ultimate Weddings

Your fantasies *can* come to life on your wedding day. So many couples now are planning the Ultimate Celebration, going all out and incorporating the best of everything with style, sophistication, and wit. The Ultimate Wedding is elegance and opulence defined, but always accomplished in good taste. And . . . those who have been married before can plan the Ultimate Wedding with as much flair as the first-time bride and groom.

One of the most memorable Ultimate Weddings of our time, of course, was that of Prince Charles and Lady Diana Spencer. All the elements of this royal event—from designer dresses to horse-drawn carriages—put romance and formality back in the nuptial spotlight. More recently, a magnificent celebration took place in several rooms of the Metropolitan Museum of Art (including the Temple of Dendur) in New York City. What made it Ultimate? Perhaps it was the fifty thousand French roses, the ten-foot-tall wedding cake covered with sculpted sugar flowers, the gold-dipped magnolia leaves decorating the tables, or the dance floor that was hand painted just for the night. Perhaps, too, it was the fact that all the guests knew that this unbelievably fabulous occasion could never, *ever* be repeated.

A fantasy wedding requires time, energy, imagination, and expertise. Sometimes it also requires money, although most of the ideas in this chapter can be modified to suit any budget. Explore the myriad possibilities for orchestrating an Ultimate Wedding. There are inventive ideas to inspire you and, more important, practical advice on how to get it all done. We know you're not competing for the Cecil B. de Mille award for your grand production; still, you want an occasion that is both regal and real, for a wedding party and guests whose first priority is to have a great time . . . together.

The Ultimate Site

A dazzling site will certainly set the tone for an Ultimate Wedding—something grand and glamorous that will motivate you and your groom to think in creative and expansive terms. The options are virtually limitless, but much depends on the size of your wedding guest list and your budget. Some wonderful sites to consider, from the expected to the offbeat, are:

- ballrooms, hotels
- tennis clubs, country clubs
- castles, mansions, historic houses
- farms, apple orchards, ranches
- botanical and winter gardens
- resorts
- art galleries, museums
- cultural centers, dance studios
- university chapels
- theaters, auditoriums
- boats, barges, trains, hot-air balloons
- discos, nightclubs
- parks, fairgrounds
- libraries
- lofts
- racetracks
- roofs, observation decks, terraces
- deserts, canyons, mountaintops

Each location will have its own unique attraction. One couple built a temporary altar with bales of hay in front of an old barn. Another married in an 1860 adobe-style church located in "Old Tucson," a

movie studio in Arizona. With each individual location come different regulations and fee schedules.
Some site owners will insist upon the use of their
own caterers; others will allow you to bring your
own. Some have kitchens for only warming the food,
which must be prepared elsewhere. Empty spaces
can be appealing—your caterer adds the tables,
chairs, and decorations. At the locations, the personnel will be able to tell you how many guests they
can comfortably handle. Remember, the number of
people who can fit standing at a cocktail party is
very different from the number of people who can
comfortably squeeze in around tables at a seated
event. Some of the most popular choices in New
York City right now, for example, are the Puck
Building, the Burden Mansion, the Rutherford
House, and the New York Academy of Art. All metropolitan areas have their gems, which are booked
as much as a year or two in advance.

If your own family garden is the ultimate site,
you'll want a large tent. Choose one of the exciting
new shapes now available. Tents can be beautifully
decorated, draped, and lighted—even air condi-
tioned or heated—so even a bad weather report
won't spoil the day.

Hotels are, of course, set up to handle weddings.
Make the hotel ballroom come alive with your choice
of flowers and greenery, food, music, and drink.
One couple transformed an otherwise sterile cube
into a holiday fantasy with eight Christmas trees
surrounded by pots full of white narcissus. Another
placed lofty vases on every table, each brimming
with tall branches in bloom, then hung garlands
from the ceiling for a springtime feast. Touches like
these create an atmosphere of merriment from which
all good vibes flow. Hotels suggest their house band,
florist, standard menu, and wine list. But you have
already decided that your wedding cannot be inter-
changeable with hundreds of others. Your unique
ideas and special extras are important to you, so discuss them with the hotel banquet managers during
your first appointment to see the site. How accom-
modating will they be? Can you bring in your own
cases of wine (vintage year of your birth)? How

much is their corkage fee, based on current prices? Can you install marbleized columns to decorate the room? Will management okay the two live swans (symbolizing monogamy) you want swimming at the reception? Will they settle for doves instead? What about the New Orleans–style jazz band you hope to hire in place of their fox-trot group? Ask questions to determine how cooperative the hotel will be from beginning to end, and how much that cooperation depends upon using their services.

The Ultimate Invitation

An Ultimate Wedding invitation lets guests know that *this* is a wedding they won't want to miss! One bride had her invitations delivered in person by her groomsmen, along with a hand-tied bouquet of fresh flowers. Guests at a medieval theme wedding had scrolled parchment invitations delivered by a costumed herald. Another couple sent guests a musical invitation, bedecked with lace, ribbons, and tulle— which played the couple's favorite song when it was opened. Invitations etched on glass and engraved on sterling silver plaques promise an elegant event.

(Contact American Crafts Enterprises, PO Box 10, New Paltz, NY 12561, the marketing branch of the American Craft Museum, for a listing of the artists who participate in ACE fairs around the country. *Crafts Report*, PO Box 1992, Wilmington, DE 19888, a monthly publication for crafts professionals, features a want-ad section that lists crafts people available for commissioned work.)

The Ultimate Dress

An ultimate dress has special flair. It could be a $30,000 designer dress completely made of antique Brussels lace; a custom-made white bridal minidress with a ''train'' of tulle from the headdress; or a backless, sleeveless, partly transparent sheath like that worn by model Elle Macpherson on her wedding day. It may have a long, conservative look for the religious ceremony—then lightened up with a skirt that's detachable from above the knee. It can make a personal statement in a subtle way, with lace appliqués from a grandmother's gown sewn onto the bodice. First seen in a head-turning walk down the aisle, it sets a dramatic tone for the festivities.

The Ultimate Music

If you and your groom move to the beat of a different drummer, you'll want your wedding music to reflect your special preferences. According to most experts, music *makes* the party—so be choosy. There are two separate musical moods: music for the ceremony and reception sound.

"Here Comes the Bride" (the "Bridal Chorus" from Wagner's *Lohengrin*), is always popular, but for the Ultimate Wedding, you may prefer walking to the strains of Bach, Handel, or Mozart. The music of a complete symphony orchestra or small string quartet or chamber music group may substitute for the traditional organ. An entire glee club lifted their voices at one joyful ceremony. Another couple incorporated this special wedding gift into their ceremony: an organ and trumpet voluntary written just for the two of them by a relative who is also a classical musician and published composer. The choice of recessional music is even more personal; James Brown's "I Feel Good" is as easily heard today as Beethoven's "Ode to Joy."

Your Ultimate Wedding might include hymns by a female vocalist, a folk Mass, African drums to herald the ceremony—or a professional opera singer, like Kiri Te Kanawa, who treated guests to a solo at Prince Charles's wedding. At the reception, welcome entering guests with a violin ensemble or chamber music. The adventurous sound of Irish folk songs, reggae, mariachis, or bluegrass fiddlers will signal to guests that this couple is indeed unique. A hint of the honeymoon destination can come across as well, in the strains of "I Love Paris" or "I Left My Heart in San Francisco." Because the style of the music needn't remain static throughout the evening, guests can switch from Cole Porter tunes to sambas to rock. Be prepared, however, to hire two different bands to do this, for not all musicians are this versatile. When choosing a band, follow this advice:

1. Talk with the band leader. Find out how he or she operates, what is his or her style of music, what

type of information is needed from you, how many requests, etc.

2. Determine how involved you want him or her to be at the reception. Some band leaders act as masters of ceremonies, announcing the first dances, the progression of courses, the cutting of the cake. You may prefer a leader who is more discreet.

3. When you have found a band you like, draw up a contract to secure its services. Make sure that the contract specifies that the members of the band you heard will be the same as those who will come to play at your party. List the leader and names of band members. Specify the number of hours musicians will play, define what is meant by "continual music," determine how long their breaks will be, and state how much the overtime fee will be if the party runs later than expected.

To trip the light fantastic (without stepping on any toes), try dance lessons in the spirit of the music you've chosen. Classes are a welcome release from any pressures during the engagement period, and when you're through, you and your fiancé will look like the "ultimate" couple, Fred and Ginger, on the dance floor. Dancing schools teach traditional ethnic dances, too, and equip couples to tango and also to amaze their friends with the samba, tarantella, flamenco, Greek handkerchief dance, horah, and square-dancing steps on their wedding day.

The Ultimate Procession

Your ultimate walk down the aisle can be short or long—but these should be the most memorable steps of your life. One bride and her dad walked for the equivalent of three blocks just to get down the "aisle"—a long grassy path between two rows of majestic chestnut trees on her family's property. This aisle was covered with a white cloth runner. Another sentimental bride walked on "memories" as a flower girl entered first, scattering dried flower petals from the many bouquets her groom had given her during their courtship. Brides have walked down long staircases in antebellum mansions, reached the altar by way of bridges built over swimming pools, even stepped from behind a backdrop of *The Mar-*

riage of Figaro to walk down the aisle. What's most important—to arrive poised and on time, ready to say the most important words of the day.

The Ultimate Keepsakes and Favors

For the Ultimate Wedding, couples search for the finest and most meaningful keepsakes and favors. A monogrammed communion wine chalice from Steuben was the perfect keepsake for one couple. A two-handled French silver *coupe de mariage* used at the reception becomes a family heirloom, as might an engraved sterling silver cake knife purchased for a cake-cutting ceremony.

Favors for guests can be personal, even extravagant. Consider these ultimate ideas:

• A custom fragrance blended just for the occasion. It is worn by the bride or groom, named after them, and placed in crystal or silvery limited edition flacons at each guest's place.

• Solid gold, sterling silver, or silver-plated long-stemmed roses—one for each guest.

• A bottle of vintage wine from the wedding year, relabeled with the names of the bridal couple and year.

• A silver plate, tray, chalice, or crystal star—engraved with a family crest or a crest newly designed for the couple, based on their interests or family backgrounds.

• Consult your own tastes: a piece of porcelain or an Italian tile, with your names and wedding date, makes a beautiful favor.

• A fine crystal piece or ceramic objects representing your interests.

• A fine writing instrument, such as a Tiffany sterling silver pen engraved with the wedding date.

• Place cards or menu cards at your wedding could be inserted into sterling silver picture frames for guests to take home. These could be heart-shaped or geometric, as you choose.

• Halcyon Days, an English company, makes a different hand-enameled copper box each year. One from your wedding year makes a unique, collectible favor.

The Ultimate Attendants' Gifts

You and your groom will want to give your attendants something they will treasure to commemorate your ultimate affair, such as:

• Signet rings with their initials. Inside, have the wedding date engraved and "Thanks."

• An item for their collection (something different for each attendant): an antique perfume bottle, porcelain statuette, music box.

• A "thank-you" trip, so the whole wedding party can enjoy a postwedding vacation too! Consider round-trip airline tickets, reservations at a country inn, a relaxing spa weekend.

• A pair of pearl or diamond earrings, tie pins for the men.

• A bridesmaid's bouquet, dried and framed by your florist ahead of time, on a plaque with their name and the wedding date.

The Ultimate Food

The Ultimate Wedding does not settle for ordinary food, since visual presentation is as important as taste. Select colorful courses and a variety of textures and shapes. Food is abundant at Ultimate Weddings: guests may consume the equivalent of *three* meals, beginning with a lavish hors d'oeuvres buffet, including separate stations for oysters, smoked salmon, caviar, crudités, and international foods—such as sushi, pasta, carved roast beef. This is followed by an elegant, seated dinner of three to five courses—as many as you wish—with appropriate wines and champagnes and a menu at every place setting. And finally—before the cake—a stunning dessert buffet (the Viennese table) is presented, accompanied by cordials and espresso. Throughout the evening, champagne and wine flows.

Think of wedding food in terms of its meaning. A caterer can replicate your favorite recipes. The oysters and poached salmon that were served at one Ultimate Wedding represented the food served on the couple's first date. A vegetarian couple can challenge the chef to create delicious dishes, from purple potatoes and fennel to artichoke hearts. Regional or ethnic foods such as goat cheese and smoked trout or sushi, and lobster with black bean sauce pay tribute to the couple's heritage.

A favorite restaurant large enough to accommodate you and your guests may be a festive reception site. Make sure, however, that the staff can manage the same wonderful food *en masse* that they normally serve to small groups.

Finding a caterer you like and whose style appeals to you may take some time—but food is so important to the success of any wedding reception. Here are some tried-and-true rules:

• DO ask everyone you know for recommendations. If you've been to a wedding recently and enjoyed the meal, ask the bride for the name of her caterer.

• DON'T forget to discuss tableware and presentation, as well as food. Caterers are usually in charge not only of the food but also of renting tables, linen, china, glass, and silver. (Price the rentals to see if it would be less costly for you to rent tableware directly from the rental company.)

• DO interview *several* caterers before making a final decision.

• DON'T choose a caterer who doesn't understand your fantasy. Unless he or she is on your wavelength, you'll be disappointed with the results. For example, if your Ultimate Wedding will not be complete without a smorgasbord or other ethnic food, you'll need a caterer capable of handling this request. Furthermore, if the caterer envisions everything "en croute," while you dream of California cuisine, start interviewing again.

• DO think about the taste and style of the meal you want *before* you settle on a caterer or you may find yourself talked into something that isn't really right for you. (Sushi may be "in," but if you hate seafood, why bother?)

• DON'T neglect service issues. A caterer must properly staff the party. Guests at an Ultimate Wedding expect attentive service from waiters and bartenders. Negotiate how many will handle the buffet and how many will pass hors d'oeuvres. Two to three waiters per table will be the most efficient, but expensive. Decide on a timetable and match it to your budget. Will the meal be served in the French manner (the waiters wear formal wear and white gloves, and present each guest's meal from large silver serving platters at each table); in the "nouvelle manner" (meals are plated in the kitchen and served); or buffet style?

• DO sign a contract. Once you've researched and selected a caterer and a menu, protect yourself against any possible changes or unforeseen events. A contract must specify everything on which you have agreed. The agreement should include the name of the chef who will work for you, the complete menu, the cake flavor(s) and topper, the liquors provided, the number of waiters promised, the waiters' attire, and the policy on "seconds," as well as any provisions for special vegetarian or restricted meals. Certain foods should be listed by weight (filet mignon, for example) so you know the size of the servings. A gratuity and tax should be stipulated as well.

The Ultimate Wines

The wines and champagnes served at your reception should be given equal thought. Wines from the years of your births or the year that you met are excellent choices. Show your true colors with a wine from your ethnic past: Italian, Spanish, German, French, Australian. Have the champagne served by white-gloved waiters carrying silver trays. One bride's rehearsal dinner for eighty was set up in a wine cellar. Guests sat at candlelit tables surrounded by enormous kegs and, of course, they drank wine, in keeping with the "spirit" of the place. (There also was, of course, transportation to take everyone home.) Sparkling rosé wines are popular, bubbling up in tulip glasses and punch bowls. If you desire something special, either let your caterer know what you want—so he or she can provide it—or tell him or her that the wines will come from your parents' cellar. If your caterer supplies the wines, champagnes, and other liquors, make sure information about these spirits is included in your catering contract and that brand names are listed where appropriate.

The Ultimate Cake

The cake at an Ultimate Wedding should be extraordinary—both in taste and appearance. Many cake decorators today are artists who can design edible masterpieces, sculpting flowers from icing or sugar paste; rolling fondant icing smooth as glass; creating delicate lattice or string work; or replicating details of the bride's dress (lace, ribbons, tulle) in icing. One Ultimate Wedding cake looked like a stack of beautifully wrapped gift boxes, another like tiers of woven baskets brimming with flowers. Many couples are also personalizing their cakes, as Sarah Ferguson and Prince Andrew did on their 240-pound wedding fruitcake, with symbols of polo, ships, and aircraft; the bride's village home; and their entwined initials on each of its five tiers. At the wedding of a woman who wrote romance novels, the cake was topped by a ''book'' on which her and her groom's names were written. You might want to have a traditional bride's cake and express yourself on the groom's cake instead. At the wedding of a groom who is an avid golfer, the groom's cake was a miniature golf course on which a round was being played by miniature figures. Along the edge of the course were the good wishes: ''May your marriage be better than par!'' Have the groom's cake sliced and boxed for guests to take home.

Ultimate Wedding cakes taste as wonderful as they look. Pick your favorite flavor: white chocolate, cheesecake, mousse cake, Grand Marnier—anything goes. Or, if you can't decide, have a different flavor in every tier. Display your cake creation in a prominent spot, where guests can admire it—perhaps on a table decorated with fresh flowers.

The Ultimate Flowers

When guests at one Ultimate Wedding entered the hotel ballroom at the start of the reception, they saw hundreds of thousands of rose petals carpeting the floor. On the tables, topiary trees laced with tiny white lights stood dramatically as centerpieces. Delicate smilax vines and hoya flowers were tied around each of the white linen napkins atop the elegant white and gold-rimmed china plates.

Arrangements like these make a statement. A floral designer will not only help select your flowers but can decorate whole rooms in floral splendor—deftly adding ribbons, garlands, baskets, and unusual floral ensembles to the scene. Designers often buy directly from floral markets to obtain the freshest flowers available for your wedding day. Bring the outdoors inside for a greenhouse effect—even in the middle of winter. Ficus trees, vines, wreaths, and trellises can transform an indoor reception site into a spring garden. For the autumn months, consider cornucopia centerpieces spilling over with seasonal yellow squash, miniature orange pumpkins, golden chrysanthemums, or red and yellow burnished leaves.

The flowers you carry should be equally important. At the Ultimate Wedding, a bride might carry a large and lush bouquet of white lilies, French tulips, and peonies to balance her full-skirted ball gown. Many brides choose bouquets bursting with color—vibrant yellow roses and deep green leaves—coordinated with her attendants. A red-headed bride might choose flowers in shades of peach, while a dark brunette might find brilliant red roses dramatic. A petite bride may prefer the simple silhouette of a single bloom, such as a white calla lily. Maids' bouquets need harmonize only with their dresses. One bride's bold statement: lavish pink roses blended with orange poppies. Or pair pink peonies with lavender hydrangea for a fresh spring look. Flowers and foliage may even be part of the wedding outfit. Brides are draping garlands of ivy or boas of flowers across their shoulders and waists, weaving ivy into their headpieces, and using colorful blossoms as part of their bodices. Flowers *do* create an Ultimate Wedding atmosphere, so be as generous as possible in their use.

The Ultimate Special Touches

Entertainment. Professional entertainment adds a festive spirit to your unique celebration. Consider mimes, acrobats, jousting contests—standard events at wedding celebrations in the Middle Ages. At one wedding celebration recently, ballerinas performed a scene for the bridal couple. Have professional dancers demonstrate a thrilling rendition of the tango or fox trot.

Vows, written or personalized by bride and groom, express the commitment of some couples more accurately—and more excitingly—than standard vows. One couple, of Spanish descent with many Spanish-speaking relatives in attendance at their ceremony, spoke their vows first in English, then in Spanish. (Their invitation and program were also printed in two languages.) Another couple had dear friends and family write and read a portion of the service, stating their support for the married couple.

A wedding canopy, under which the two of you exchange your vows, adds a symbolic and elegant touch to your day. In Jewish ceremonies, the *huppah* symbolizes the home the married couple will share— but any religion can incorporate this welcoming idea. A canopy is a personal expression of your style; it may be made all of flowers—for example, hundreds of yellow roses for a golden arch—or it may be a hand-painted silk canopy or heavily embroidered velvet.

Candlelight can bring warmth and sophistication to evening weddings. At a winter wedding after sunset, candles can be used atop pedestals decorated with flowers and bows or placed in majestic silver candelabra. At a summer wedding, candles placed throughout the reception site will cast a brighter glow as the sun goes down. Candles may be all white or match the colors of your wedding. They might line the walk from the church to the reception site or outline the steps of the church or synagogue. (Check fire safety regulations first.) Bridesmaids might carry romantic lanterns to light your wedding walk. Votive candles, placed in sand-filled terra-cotta jars, will glow throughout the reception in true southwestern style. Candles can also be used symbolically. A couple might light a Unity Candle together as their lives are becoming one, then keep the candle and rekindle the flame on each anniversary.

Balloons add a festive touch. One couple released three hundred cream, gold, peach, and turquoise helium balloons into the air outside their wedding reception. Each balloon had a scroll attached, with the names and wedding date of the couple, enabling anyone who found one of the balloons to share in the day with them. (Check laws: Some states may prohibit this, since balloons can be harmful to the environment and wildlife.) Helium balloons can also be tied to chairs, posts, or even floral arrangements for a buoyant look and festive ambience. Ceilings can be decorated with hundreds of balloons—in multiple colors or all in white and silver.

Wedding drama is achieved with an all-white theme. Imagine white limousines, white tablecloths, white tuxedos, white invitations lettered in gold or silver, guests in white silks and satins, silvery centerpieces, the golden glow of white candles. Sometimes the addition of one color is striking: peach roses, for example, for romantic bouquets, or topiaries made of brilliant red roses for each table. The drama of black caught the fancy of one actress, who had her reception tables draped in black satin and surrounded by silver chairs; centerpieces were four-foot-tall silver-and-white arrangements composed of gardenias, orchids, and willows with ostrich feathers pluming out at the top.

Theatrical effects can breathe new life into parties. Mimes can welcome your guests, and comedians and clowns can tickle their funny bones. Plan a fireworks display to dazzle late-nighters or explore the possibility of a laser show to light up the skies. Hire a plane to sky write your names above a beach or poolside reception. Bring human mannequins—actors dressed and posed in period costumes—to add authenticity to the historical theme of your wedding.

Romantic arrivals and getaways add to the excitement as well. A horse-drawn carriage, gondola, or helicopter can be the ultimate way to honor the occasion or start your honeymoon. One couple and their twenty-six-member wedding party flew from their wedding site in New York City to the bride's house in Sands Point, New York, where the reception was being held. The 350 guests followed (more slowly, of course) on a "party bus," where they found snack bags with elegant sandwiches and fruit on their seats; champagne was served. Other couples have scooted off on motorbikes, drifted off in boats with "Just Married" sails, motored off in antique cars, and sailed off in hot-air balloons. Your transportation is limited only by your imagination and the theme of your Ultimate Wedding.

6.
Theme Weddings

The invitation, shaped like a tennis racquet, read "Here's the score: love/love for John Davidson and Patty Hill. Please join us at our wedding, Shaker Gymnasium, Lancaster, Pennsylvania, June 3, 11 A.M. An outdoor reception immediately following at Dexter Playing Fields." Both sports fanatics, the bride and groom are coaches at a large high school. They felt a sports theme wedding would be the ideal way for them to tie the knot. They married on the basketball court, beautifully decorated with potted palms and tubs of white mums, as guests sat in the bleachers. Flowers filled the basketball hoops at either end. The outdoor buffet following the ceremony was held on the very field Patty used daily for field hockey practice. Guests received whistles with tags attached, reading "It's official! John and Patty, June 3, 1989." The couple also had baseball card favors made up, picturing the two of them on the front with their vital statistics on the back: dates of birth, how they met, first date, occupations, hobbies. The ushers received autographed baseballs from their favorite teams; the bridesmaids were given silver tennis-racquet charms. The bridal party chipped in and got Patty and John season tickets to the Philadelphia Phillies.

Many couples favor Theme Weddings because they want their big day to be both innovative and

personal. You can incorporate your theme throughout the wedding and reception, where appropriate,
as long as you don't belabor the point. Following
are a number of themes—from Valentine's Day to
Christmas, nautical to military, historical to ethnic—
to consider, plus information on how to plan and
stage a Theme Wedding to maximum effect.

THE MILITARY WEDDING

For couples in the armed forces, the Military Wedding can be a dramatic way to honor military status
with a beautiful celebration. The style of the wedding is dictated by "tradition" rather than strict
laws, so a great deal of flexibility is allowed. Invitations might have gold-braided edges or a pen-and-
ink illustration of crossed swords. The ceremony can
take place in a church or synagogue or in the chapel
at the base. Who can marry at a military chapel? A
graduate of a military academy, either active or re-
tired; a child of a graduate; a member of the faculty
or staff. During the ceremony, most couples display
the American flag and/or the standards of their units.
Grooms should wear full ceremonial dress, including white gloves and saber (Army, Marines) or
sword (Navy, Coast Guard). Military decorations,
not boutonnieres, are worn. A bride in one of the
armed services may marry in full uniform or in a
traditional wedding gown. If she chooses the uniform, she may still carry a bouquet. Sabers or swords
can be used for the cake-cutting ceremony and, of
course, are raised by an honor guard to create the
arch through which the bridal couple pass. Those
carrying sabers or swords must be in uniform. Members of the honor guard may also be the couple's
attendants. The arch of swords symbolizes a safe
passage into matrimony and is usually done just
outside the chapel doors. At the center, the couple
kisses, and the ones in uniform should salute the
honor guard.

Invitations should be addressed according to military protocol. If the rank is above captain in the
Army, or lieutenant, senior grade, in the Navy, the
title appears before the name (Captain Marjorie

Rider, United States Army). Otherwise, the title is given after the name, such as Marvin Black, Ensign, United States Navy. For help with sorting out the dos and don'ts of military etiquette in a particular division, contact the protocol officer.

A DAY IN THE COUNTRY WEDDING

Rose petals are sprinkled down the center of the grassy aisle to form a natural "runner" for the bride and her father. A gentle breeze is blowing across the sun-warmed fields. The ceremony is held in front of a bubbling fountain or under a canopy of flowers. The bride, in white eyelet, carries a hand-tied bouquet of cornflowers, peonies, and ivy. Wide, low baskets filled with garden flowers enhance the country theme.

Today's Country Weddings are not the barefoot-and-berry celebrations of the 1960s. Stylish and elegant, they may take place inside a gazebo or by a goldfish pond. They may be held at a quaint settlers' mission in the West, a renovated ghost town, or the family horse ranch.

The bride might carry a bouquet of white roses and stephanotis, or loosely tied wildflowers or sheaves of wheat, held together with crisp white ribbon. (Wheat symbolizes hope for a rich, full life.) A nosegay of herbs is traditional at Country Weddings, often in combination with other flowers and foliage. Choose among rosemary (remembrance), sage (wisdom), thyme (sacrifice), ivy (fidelity), and four-leaf clovers (good luck). Centerpieces for the reception tables can display the simple beauty of a vegetable still life.

The country atmosphere continues at tables, set on the greenest grass, skirted and flounced with white eyelet or linen, and surrounded by white wicker chairs. Or, for rustic charm, they may be decorated with red gingham and pots of yellow sunflowers.

Collections of antique or modern quilts are colorful decorations for a country theme. Display your own, if you collect them. Or borrow new ones to skirt a table or buffet. (You don't want an antique to take too much of a beating.) To create a keepsake with a sense of history, ask each guest to contribute a square of fabric, and send them all to a custom quiltmaker, along with the dimensions of your bed. Over the centuries, couples were often given quilts by their bridal parties. Each member designed and embroidered a square that reflected something about the couple; today it might be hobbies and interests—from fishing to horseback riding. Your guests might be inspired to do the same.

An informal country theme conjures up visions of hearty food: robust potluck suppers, baskets of freshly baked breads, fried chicken, Swiss steak, warm corn muffins, pasta salads, chicken wings, garden-ripe tomatoes, fresh corn. Tiers of carrot cake can be decorated with fresh flowers, cascades of pulled sugar grapes, or sugar butterflies, cut and served on floral china plates. At one informal Country Wedding that took place on a cattle ranch in Texas, the groom's cake was shaped like a cowboy boot.

Guests can enjoy hayrides, or dance to a bluegrass band or country and Western music. And everybody loves a square dance (with the best caller in town). At a Western-style wedding, a cowboy boot substituted for the bride's bag as the best man passed it around to collect money for the newlyweds. At the end of one such wedding, the couple rode off on a getaway tractor. Others have chosen a surrey with a fringe on top or a covered wagon. Birdseed, laced with dried petals from the garden and kernels of wheat, rained down to wish them good luck.

A DAY ON THE OCEAN WEDDING

The sun is just beginning its slow descent over the water as the yacht holding bride, groom, and 150 guests pulls effortlessly away from the dock. Cocktails are being served as a trio of wind instruments plays classical music. Suddenly, there are three sharp blasts from the ship's horn. Everyone files out on deck to watch the couple say their vows as the sun finally dips into the sea in a burst of orange and gold. After the ceremony, a sumptuous buffet appears, representing the wonders of the sea—fresh shrimp, caviar, raw oysters, grilled halibut, and loaves of bread baked in the shapes of seahorses, starfish, and dolphins. Fresh fruit surrounds a large ice sculpture of a marlin. The caterer's team of waiters is dressed in crisp nautical attire and white sneakers. Captain's hats are presented to the parents of the bride and groom along with a humorous toast from the newlyweds. Thin silver whistles are given to all on board as party favors. Atop the cake sits a small pair of hand-painted lobsters, their claws entwined, made of porcelain. This nautical theme wedding is perfect for sailors and landlubbers alike.

New York City couples often say "I do" aboard the many boats that tour the island of Manhattan, giving guests sweeping views of the skyline and the Statue of Liberty as they dine and dance.

One scuba-diving couple took the nautical theme to extremes and married under water. The officiant, however, stayed on dry land and communicated via special microphone. Afterward, the couple and guests shared a cake with two scuba divers on top. Other ideas for a Day on the Ocean Wedding: Marry on a dock, at lakeside, or by the seashore. A boathouse or yacht club provides a safe haven and an authentic setting. If you're planning to be married on board ship, remember that ship's captains can't marry anyone—so make sure you have an authorized officiant with you, or marry legally at the city hall before having a ship's captain unofficially "remarry" you on board.

The sea theme can be brought indoors as well, with these creative ideas:

• Top the wedding cake with seashells or a half shell holding a tiny bride and groom.

• Dress child attendants in sailor outfits.

• Name tables for ships instead of using numbers (sailfish, sloop, dinghy).

• Design invitations to match the theme.

• Place ships inside bottles on the bride and groom's table.

• Fill open ceramic clamshells with votive candles for reception centerpieces.

• Have a special groom's cake designed. One

water-worshiping couple who married near a bay in Florida baked the groom's cake in the shape of a marlin.

• Give out hand-cast ceramic shells, with the couple's names etched inside, for wedding favors.

• Place candied almonds wrapped in netting inside shell dishes for each guest.

• Fill lobster traps with flowers for creative centerpieces.

• Create watermelon ''boats'' hollowed out to carry a cargo of fruit salad.

• Request the band to play ''Swanee River'' or ''Yellow Submarine,'' or give them sheet music of sea shanties to learn in advance.

A STEP BACK IN TIME

The sun is shining brightly upon the garden outside the southern antebellum home where the wedding is about to start. The ancient magnolia trees of this old cotton plantation are all in bloom, lanterns hang from every post, arrangements of gardenias grace the reception tables. It's the 1990s, but it could as easily be a pre–Civil War movie set. Now bridesmaids in hoop skirts, carrying parasols, begin the processional up the long brick walk leading to the portico of the mansion. The bride, in a Scarlett O'Hara–style wedding dress and garden hat with sweeping brim, follows them up the aisle on her father's arm. After the dining and dancing, the bride and groom cut an extraordinary cake—a replica of a white-pillared southern mansion. Finally, the couple leave the party in an old-fashioned horse and carriage covered with flowers and ribbons.

Period weddings are gaining in popularity. If you and your groom have always thought of a particular time of history as romantic, bring this era to life at your wedding. Your choice of a special site, wedding attire, food, and favors can reflect your historical theme. Invitations set the tone. One couple who married at a Renaissance fair, for example, sent each guest an invitation in script on rolled parchment.

Renaissance fairs, which take place at different times during the year, feature food, music, and entertainment of the period. Mandolins play, jousting tournaments are scheduled, and a medieval meal— complete with hearty roasts and spiced wine—is served on trenchers ("place mats" made of bread that soak up the juices) as couples tie the knot, often in Renaissance outfits. East Coast brides should call the New York Renaissance Festival (Sterling Forest, Tuxedo, NY; 212-645-1630). West Coast brides can contact the Renaissance Pleasure Faire (The Living History Center, Novato, CA; 415-892-0937).

The Victorian period is also a popular theme for weddings. In a bustled gown with a high neck and lots of ivory lace, a bride can say her wedding vows in a Victorian garden. For the reception, turn-of-the-century foods, claret, and a string quartet playing the classics complete the picture. (Contact the Victorian Society, 219 South 6th Street, Philadelphia, PA 19106, for more ideas.)

One bride decided on a 1920s theme after she saw an old wedding photo of her grandparents, who married in 1922. She arrived at the wedding site in an antique burgundy and white Rolls Royce, wearing a knee-length silk chemise with a jagged hem and plunging back, covered with silver and crystal beading. At the reception, a pianist played 1920s tunes like "Button Up Your Overcoat," and the guests danced the Charleston. When the couple cut the cake, they kissed over the original cake topper used by her grandparents and a plate from her mother's service.

After their ceremony in a gazebo, one couple took guests on a paddle-boat ride up the Mississippi, complete with a Dixieland band dressed in Old South costumes and the zestiest Cajun food.

A bride from the Northeast married at historic Sturbridge Village, wearing a Federalist-style gown with lace petticoats. Colonial weddings have significance for many U.S. families, but especially if the bride hails from any of the thirteen colonial states, or if the wedding takes place over the Fourth of July or Thanksgiving weekends. The reception site can be decorated in Early American simplicity, with waiters and waitresses in colonial costumes serving turkey with all the trimmings. Pewter jewelry is traditional for the bridesmaids as thank-you gifts. The couple registers for pewter items with an antique flair. Another Early American custom to observe: The bride pins a small pouch to her wedding petticoat containing a tiny sliver of bread, cloth, wood, and a single dollar bill tucked inside—meant to ensure enough food, clothes, shelter, and money for the future.

Original fresh ideas for your favorite historical period can be found in the library, from historical societies, and from museums. Costume books show how women wore their hair and what the fashions were. Discover modes of transportation, popular songs, sayings, and games you didn't even know existed. For guest favors, fill old-fashioned Victorian hat boxes with candies. Or heap heart-shaped boxes painted by a local artist with candy hearts or kisses. All of these ideas will make a period wedding dream a reality.

SEASONAL THEMES

Just as the bride and groom complete their late-evening vows and are pronounced husband and wife, fireworks light up the sky. In time with the resounding salvos, the orchestra—assembled outdoors with the bridal party and guests—plays the "1812 Overture." Once the show is over, guests are handed sparklers to carry as they walk together across the open fields to a restored Revolutionary War inn. At tables, miniature American flags wave from the centerpieces, and ale is served in red, white, and blue mugs bearing the names and wedding date of the bridal couple. A Fourth of July Wedding is under way.

You may want to marry near a holiday and give seasonal charm to your day. Gather your families together for several festive occasions, and celebrate your families' traditions. Below are just a few ideas.

Christmas
• Choose velvet dresses for maids and flower girls, and velvet suits for ring bearers.
• Arrange for a group of youngsters to come car-

oling at the reception; pass out holiday song sheets to everyone.

• Decorate tiny Christmas trees with take-home favors and put one at each guest's place.

• Play yuletide tunes during the cocktail hour.

• Serve green mint frappé drinks topped with red maraschino cherries after dinner.

• Dip apples on sticks in white chocolate and decorate them with a yuletide theme.

• Carry a white muff decorated with poinsettias.

• Have bridesmaids carry floral wreath bouquets with tiny silver bells. As the just-married bride and groom kiss, all can jingle their approval.

• Decorate table centerpieces with pinecones.

• Hang mistletoe over the cake and kiss during the cake-cutting ceremony.

• Give guests Christmas tree ornaments, with your names and wedding date, as favors.

Fourth of July
• Choose a dress with eighteenth-century flair.

• Set tables with red, white, and blue cloths.

• Serve an all-American barbecue.

• Top off the meal with fabulous ice cream desserts.

• Plan for a grand finale of sparklers and fireworks.

• Top a tall cake with flags and more sparklers.

• Marry at a location with Revolutionary War history.

• Have bridesmaids wear red; groomsmen, blue.

Easter
• Pile brightly painted eggs and spring flowers in Easter baskets for centerpieces.

• Think of rabbits everywhere—even a bunny bride and groom on the cake.

• Use a rainbow color scheme, with each bridesmaid dressed in a different pastel.

• Wear a glamorous ''Easter bonnet'' and an airy garden party dress.

• Invite guests to play croquet or lawn bowling.

• Remember the children—this is a family day, after all. Arrange an Easter egg hunt.

Valentine's Day

• Choose a gown with subtle pink or red accents—tiny satin rosettes on bodice and sleeves, a pale pink ruffle adorning the hem, a blush-colored silk sheath overlaid with white lace.

• Dress bridesmaids in romantic gowns of ruby velvet, rose chiffon, or pink satin.

• On wedding morning, send a bouquet of heart-shaped balloons to your groom—perhaps delivered by a singing Cupid in a red leotard, carrying an arrow.

• Write a love poem for your groom; before the ceremony, have your maid of honor deliver it to him.

• Present each bridesmaid with a heart-shaped music box that plays a romantic tune; a heart-shaped silver locket or earrings; a heart-shaped tin of bath oils, bubble bath, scented candles.

• Have your florist create bridal bouquets and centerpieces with red, white, and pink blooms: peppermint-striped parrot tulips, sweetheart roses, cyclamen, holly berries, ranunculus, stock, bouvardia, calla lilies, stephanotis, gardenias, phalaenopsis orchids.

• Order a tiered, heart-shaped cake decorated with delicate icing flowers, topped with a Cupid.

• Write guests' table assignments on Victorian-style valentines.

• For guests, order heart-shaped chocolates and set them at each reception place, as reception favors; place a red rose on each plate.

• Thank your parents with a heart-shaped basket filled with tea biscuits, candies, jams, exotic teas.

ETHNIC TOUCHES

A wedding celebrates our differences as well as our desire for unity. The bride from Ireland, for example, marrying a man whose parents came to the U.S. from Greece, will want to weave the two cultures together at their wedding. Customs, traditions, dances, music, and food from other parts of the world add personality to a wedding. Ask both families for ideas and family traditions, then incorporate them as you see fit. Here are some examples:

• One bride, who wanted to include a tribute to her Chinese ancestry, turned out the lights at her reception and surprised guests with an ancient ''lion and dragon dance,'' originally created to ward off evil spirits. Drums beat fiercely as a ten-foot-long lion and dragon danced around the room. The bride and groom then held up a red (the color of love and joy) envelope with good-luck money in it, and the beasts grabbed it and disappeared (temporarily!).

• The groom, a full-blooded Cherokee, and his bride, half Cherokee, chose a Native American wedding. They wore traditional wedding clothes: she was dressed in a white buckskin dress and he in tan buckskin pants with an open beaded vest. During the ceremony, they drank from a two-spouted jug to symbolize the joining of two families. Then the couple exchanged gifts of corn and venison, to show that both would be responsible for providing for the household. An American Indian bride might also honor her heritage by carrying brightly colored, dried Indian corn, with the husks attached, in place of a traditional bouquet.

One couple served French petit-heart pastries, English bishop's sweetbread, and German rosewater cookies at their reception to symbolize the joining of their heritages.

Here are some ideas from other backgrounds that the readers of *Bride's* have used at their weddings:

African Traditions

• The bride's guests line up on one side of the room, the groom's guests on the other. They then walk forward to meet in the middle and embrace, and then they switch sides. This tradition symbolizes the marriage of two families.

• Some tribes tie the bride's and groom's wrists together with braided grass. Perhaps honor your new ties with a loose chain of flowers instead.

• In Kenya, fertility necklaces and swords (traditional symbols of fertility and marriage) are given to the couple.

• In Algeria, a Jewish couple and their families dined on bread and honey at a dinner prior to the wedding ceremony. Bread represents the sustenance of life and honey its sweetness.

Arab Traditions

• Jewish and Arab women who live in Arab countries "ululate," or sing a high-pitched ritual song to express their joy for the bride.

Armenian Traditions

• Two white doves are released to signify love and happiness.

• Guests wrap the couple in a ribbon of one-dollar bills during their first dance to ensure a lifetime of good fortune together.

Austrian Traditions

• The bride weaves myrtle (the flower of life) into her veil or crown.

• The bride and groom ride to the town hall in a horse and carriage for the ceremony.

Belgian Traditions

• The bride embroiders her own name onto her bridal handkerchief, then frames and keeps it for the next family bride. Why not share this tradition with your attendants by embroidering a handkerchief for each of them?

Bermudian Traditions

• The bride's cake is a tiered fruitcake, covered with silver leaf and topped with a tiny cedar tree. The tree is then planted by the bride and groom so that it will grow along with their love.

• The groom's cake is a plain pound cake, covered with gold leaf.

• The bride and groom ride in a horse and carriage after the wedding and reception.

Bulgarian Traditions

• A "wedding tree," which is actually a branch of pine, is carried during a procession to the bride and groom's new home. It is later sold to the godfather and stripped after the wedding night.

Chinese Traditions

• Invitations, wedding dress, candles, and gift boxes are in red—the traditional color of love and joy.

• Fortune cookies are given out after the meal to bring good luck to the guests. Guests used to dine on delicacies like bear nose!

• The bride and groom drink from goblets of wine and honey, symbolically tied together with a red string.

• The bride's mother fills a purse with gold, jewelry, and money, and gives it to the bride to keep, in case of adversity.

• The couple attends a tea service after the ceremony, hosted by the groom's family. The bride, wearing a *cheong sam* (the traditional Chinese dress with a mandarin collar), arrives with her groom and a chaperone. The table is set with seaweed soup, snow peas, and vermicelli in memory of the ancestors. The couple bows to the elders present, who give them red envelopes containing money.

Cypriot Traditions

• A pig is roasted at the reception.

• The entire town is invited to the celebration.

Czechoslovakian Traditions

• Wreaths of rosemary (signifying remembrance of the bride's family, her love, and her loyalty to her husband) are woven the night before the wedding and then worn by the bride at the ceremony.

Dutch Traditions

• At a pre-wedding party, bride and groom sit on thrones under a canopy of evergreens—symbolizing the couple's everlasting love. Guests come up to offer their good wishes.

• The bride is given a traditional, six-sided wedding box engraved with allegorical figures and domestic scenes, for her personal treasures. In past centuries, the box was filled with gold ducats.

Egyptian Traditions

• A procession from the wedding to the reception is led by belly dancers, men carrying flaming swords, and people sounding long horns. Brides dress in Western wedding dress, but guests wear traditional Egyptian clothes.

English Traditions

• The bride must not allow her married name to be used before the wedding takes place, or it might never happen.

• Traditionally, the safest season to marry was between the harvest and Christmas, when food was plentiful. An old English rhyme says, "Marry in September's shine, your living will be rich and fine."

• If the couple will marry in a church, banns announcing the proposed wedding are read aloud in church on the three Sundays before the wedding. It is unlucky for the bride and groom to be present at the calling of the banns.

• Wear "something old, something new, something borrowed and something blue, and a lucky sixpence in your shoe," as in the English rhyme. If you can't find sixpence—some companies make them for brides—substitute a lucky penny.

• The wedding party walks to the church together in a procession (an age-old custom that protected the couple from jealous ex-suitors!). A flower girl leads the way, sprinkling petals along the road. This signifies a happy route through life for the bride and groom.

• Traditionally, English brides had only one adult attendant (for a witness). Today, it is still the custom to have many young bridesmaids instead of adult attendants.

• Church bells ring as the couple enter; they peal a different tune as the newlyweds exit, to scare off evil spirits.

• The newlyweds may pass through an arch of sabers or swords (for servicemen), pitchforks (for farmers), nightsticks (for policemen), or other appropriate objects.

• Old-fashioned fruitcake is served, which dates back to the days before leavening and sugar.

Finnish Traditions

• Laurel leaves (symbolizing fertility) are laid outside the town hall or church—as a bridal path.

• The bride wears a gold crown in her hair and passes it on to one of her bridesmaids, rather than tossing a bouquet. First, she is blindfolded, then the unmarried women dance around her in a circle until she places the crown. You might wear a garland of flowers at your wedding and follow this tradition, saving your wedding bouquet as a keepsake.

French Traditions

• On the wedding day, the groom may meet the bride at her house and proceed with her to the procession of guests, which walks to the church. Children may block the path with white ribbons, which the couple must cut. In a church filled with incense and flowers, the couple stand beneath a silk canopy while a bishop officiates.

• Reception tables overflow with flowers guests bring—to honor the couple's fresh beginning. Brides wear wreaths of flowers in their hair.

• Bride and groom toast each other from a two-handled silver *coupe de mariage*.

• In Brittany, the wedding party and the bride and groom drink from a glass of brandy poured over a piece of white bread, symbolic of the beginning of the "toasting" custom. (The couple get the last sip and the bread for good luck.)

• Outside the church, laurel leaves are laid down as a bridal path.

German Traditions

• During the engagement, bride and groom each wear gold bands.

• Invitations rich in artwork are sent. Or, traditionally, in the country a *Kostenbidder*, or wedding inviter, dressed in a suit decorated with flowers and ribbon, knocks on each guest's door with a stick decorated with a wreath. (He is also the toastmaster at the reception, and then introduces each guest to present their gift.) The bride and groom may invite each guest personally as well, bestowing small gifts (perhaps handkerchiefs from a basket).

• The bride's furniture was traditionally driven to her future home in a cart, with driver and playing musicians. At the threshold, the groom greeted her with a jug of beer; she gave him a pair of shoes, a shirt she spun and wove, and the key to her bridal chest.

• The bride often wears an heirloom gown, and each has her own elaborate wedding crown constructed of wire, tinsel, artificial flowers, pearls, ribbon, and pins. It is bad luck to try on someone else's crown, or take her own off before midnight, when it is replaced by a bonnet. The groom, best man, and bridesmaids then dance around the blindfolded bride. She must catch a bridesmaid (the next to marry). Married women then tie the bridal bonnet on this maid, who must dance with all of the groom's male relatives—around three lit candles on the floor. If they are not extinguished by the end of the dancing, the marriage will be smooth.

• On wedding morning, a breakfast called "morning soup" or "bridal soup" is served for guests. The groom then calls for his bride (who may be hidden for him to find) and drives her to church.

• When the couple kneels during the ceremony, the groom may kneel on the hem of the bride's gown, to symbolize that he will keep her in order. The bride may step on his foot when she rises, to reassert herself.

• At the newlywed home, the couple share a bite of bread, symbolizing that they will never be short of food. The bride is pushed to the kitchen at once; as a housewife, she must first put salt in the soup!

• The bride's mother may throw rice or dried peas over the bride; the grains that stick in her gown represent the number of expected children.

• At the reception, large red and blue checked napkins are given to guests, to take leftover food home.

• At the reception, guests throw special plates (meant for that purpose) onto the floor where the reception is held. As the groom sweeps up the broken plates, guests buy dances with the bride (the money helps pay for the honeymoon).

Greek Traditions

• The groom, *koumbaros* (the groom's godfather, best man, or an honored guest who participates in the ceremony and assists in the crowning of the bridal couple), friends, relatives, and musicians walk in a procession to the bride's house, where she is dressed by her friends. The couple then lead the procession to the church.

• In Crete, two loaves of bread are baked, decorated with flowers, tied together with white ribbon, and separated by a bottle of wine. The ribbon is cut when the couple enter the church.

• Crowns (often of orange blossoms—traditional bridal flowers that are synonymous with purity and loveliness) are placed on the bride's and groom's heads during the wedding ceremony to symbolize their entrance into the realm of marriage.

• Greek Orthodox couples take three sips of wine and circle the altar three times with the priest, to symbolize the Trinity (while guests throw rice).

• The bridegroom's friends help the bride remove her dowry and household goods to the newlywed home. The bride's mother throws a piece of raw cotton on each, symbolizing the fruits of the soil. The groom's mother may meet her at the door of her new home with a glass of honey and water; the bride must drink it so words from her lips may be sweet as honey. The remainder is smeared on the door, so strife may never enter. To symbolize the strength of her new home, a Greek bride may toss a piece of iron onto her roof.

• During the wedding, the couple dances the "Dance of Isaiah," during which they are showered with sugared almonds.

Hawaiian Traditions

• The groom wears a maile, an open-ended lei of dark green leaves, and white clothing, accented with a red sash or cummerbund. The bride wears six or seven leis of tiny white flowers around her neck and a crown of flowers in her hair.

Indian Traditions

· Minstrels fill the street with music as they escort the couple through the village.

· The bride dresses like a gilded rose—in a sari of pink or red trimmed with gold.

· At the end of the ceremony, to ward off evil, the groom's brother sprinkles flower petals on the couple's shoulders.

· The couple's hands are painted with henna swirls—beautiful ornamentation. Traditionally the bride and groom leave their handprints at the door of their marriage house—symbols of good luck and ownership. (Sephardic Jews paint the hands of the bridal couple with henna dye to ward off the evil eye.)

Irish Traditions

· *Claddagh* rings are exchanged. These traditional Irish wedding bands are formed by two hands clasping a crowned heart, symbolizing the reign of love and friendship.

· A lucky horseshoe is given to the bride and groom to keep in their home.

· A piece of fine Irish lace is sewn into the hem of the bride's gown for good luck.

· Irish folk dancers perform for guests.

· A traditional fruitcake laced with brandy or bourbon, ground almonds, golden raisins, cherries, and spice is served as the wedding cake.

Italian Traditions

· The front grille of the car is decorated with flowers to signify happy travels through life together.

· Traditional love-knot cookies are served.

· The bride is given a doll by the groom as a wedding gift.

· The groom's tie is cut up, and pieces of it are sold to guests for honeymoon money.

· Sugared almonds are given as favors or tossed at the bride and groom as confetti. In fact, the term *confetti* originates from this custom, which has been adapted in the U.S. as small bits of paper.

Jamaican Traditions

• Slices of dark wedding fruitcake laced with rum are mailed to all friends and relatives unable to attend the reception.

Japanese Traditions

• The bride and groom take nine sips of sake, a Japanese wine made from rice, in the *san-san-kudo* (three and three, nine times) ceremony, becoming husband and wife after the first one. Family members repeat this at the reception, to symbolize that they are bound together.

• Japanese brides change their clothes three or four times during the wedding. First, a white kimono is worn to show the bride's willingness to adopt the groom's family. Her head must be covered, to hide horns of jealousy. She then changes to a Western-style wedding gown. Next she dons a multicolored kimono, a *furisode*, for the reception, and finally she changes into a Western-style ball gown (optional). The groom wears a black kimono with his family crest.

• The bride's and the groom's families give elaborate favors to guests. These presents are often half the value of gifts given to the couple.

• A custom known as *sato-gaeri* (the word means ''returning to the bride's house'') often follows the wedding. The groom takes his wife to be formally introduced to his family. The following day and night, the bride introduces her groom at her family's home, after which the couple finally returns to their own home.

Korean Traditions

• A symbolic hand-painted duck or a live goose and gander (all of which mate for life) are carried in the procession as a reminder of fidelity.

• The bride and groom are lifted into the air by guests during certain parts of the reception.

Lithuanian Traditions

• The newlyweds are served a meal of wine, salt, and bread. The wine symbolizes joy, the salt is for tears, and the bread stands for work.

Mexican Traditions

• A large loop of rosary beads, symbolizing unity, is placed in a figure-eight shape around the necks of the couple after they say their vows. This same "lasso" can also be beautiful when made of entwined orange blossoms.

• Thirteen gold coins (*arras*) are given to the bride by the groom, signifying that he will support her. These become family heirlooms. The number of coins represents Jesus Christ and his 12 apostles.

• Guests make a heart-shaped circle around the bride and groom as they take their first dance.

• Godparents of the bride and groom give the couple a prayer book, rosary, and kneeling pillow for the ceremony.

Moroccan Traditions

• The bride and groom are showered with dates, figs, and raisins—symbols of fertility—instead of rice.

Norwegian Traditions

• The bride's mother prepares a thick sour-cream porridge, which is eaten during the wedding feast with pea soup, curds and whey sweetened with syrup, at 3 A.M.

• A traditional wedding cake of bread baked with white flour (which was once rare) is topped with cheese, cream, and syrup, then cut into squares. Another cake is made of almond paste, and decorated with the couple's initials.

• The bride may walk to church, wearing traditional dress and crown, with her groom, friends, relatives, a master of ceremony, and fiddler.

• The celebration lasts into the wee hours of the morning while the midnight sun still shines. At dinner, guests dine on shish kebab (which is often made with reindeer meat).

Orthodox Jewish Traditions

The bride is given a *mikvah*, or ritual bath of purification, before the wedding. She often bathes in pure rainwater.

Polish Traditions

· A gift of salted bread and sweet wine is presented to the couple, to signify the bitter and sweet in life.

· Guests pay to dance the "Dollar Dance" with the bride, who carries a small bag or purse in which to place the money. The cash is used for the honeymoon.

· The bride is serenaded before the wedding. An old Polish folk ballad is sung in which the bride is given a "bossing" about how to be a good wife.

Puerto Rican Traditions

· A bridal doll is placed on the head table at the reception.

Scottish Traditions

· Bagpipe players entertain guests before the ceremony and reception.

· The Scottish sword dance can be performed at the reception.

· The groom traditionally purchases a silver "Wedding Spune" for his bride, engraved with their initials and the wedding date.

· Church bells ring an ancient Celtic call to worship.

Spanish Traditions

· Brides once married in black silk dresses and mantillas—with orange blossoms in their hair. Grooms wore tucked shirts, hand-embroidered by their brides.

· In celebrating the event, the groom pays "ransom" to the village men with meats, wine, and delicacies, and gives the women bonbons.

· The groom gives 13 coins (the giving of *monedas* or *arras*) to the bride, symbolizing his ability to support and care for her. During the ceremony, she carries them in a special purse, or a young girl carries them on a pillow or handkerchief.

· Bride and groom wear wedding bands on the right hand.

· Wedding guests dance a *seguidillas manchegas*

dance at the reception, where each guest presents the bride with a gift.

Swedish Traditions

· To frighten away trolls (imaginary beings), bridesmaids traditionally surrounded the bride and carried strongly scented herbs. The groom sewed thyme into his clothes.

· Bride and groom may dance around a maypole.

· Traditionally, the bride would go through the wedding ceremony with her shoes untied, proceed to her honeymoon chamber, go to bed, and consummate her marriage, still wearing the untied shoes! She would sleep with the shoes dangling on her feet, hoping that they fall off by themselves during the night (an indication that she will bear children as easily as she removes her shoes).

Swiss Traditions

· Guests contribute to the couple's savings by "buying" a colored handkerchief from the junior bridesmaid, who heads the procession to the reception.

Welsh Traditions

· The bride gives her attendants myrtle (the flower of life) and instructs them to plant the cuttings. If they grow, there'll be another wedding.

· The churchyard gates are only opened after the village children are bribed with a shower of coins.

Yugoslavian Traditions

· The bridal car and the guests' cars are all decorated with flowers.

A marriage of many different backgrounds can incorporate a tribute to each. One bride danced a Norwegian waltz at her wedding (to honor her father's ancestry), followed by the groom and his mother dancing to a Spanish tune. Then they all donned hats indicating the many countries represented by the immediate family—Norway, the Philippines, Greece, Italy, Spain, and the U.S.—and

HOW TO MAKE PERFECT TEA

To brew tea for a large crowd, you'll want to make a tea concentrate first. Bring a quart of water to a full boil and pour it over two-thirds cup of loose tea. Cover and let stand for a few minutes. Then stir and strain into a teapot. (This recipe makes enough for twenty-five people.) To serve a perfect cup of tea, boil another pot of water and place it in a separate teapot. Pour about two tablespoons of the tea concentrate into a cup and then fill it the rest of the way with the hot water.

they invited guests to join in singing "It's a Small World."

THE WEDDING TEA

It's 4:00 P.M. The afternoon sun streams into the large drawing room of the British-style hunting lodge where the wedding will take place. Polished silver teapots and trays shine. Crystal sparkles. Starched white tablecloths cover the tables. A piano player tinkles the ivories on the baby grand. Scenes of fox hunts grace the walls. Scones and clotted cream are served. Strawberries and cream, à la Wimbledon, and a selection of sherries are among the British-style treats in store for guests. The timing and atmosphere are right for the Wedding Tea.

A tea-time party can be charming held indoors or out, for large or small groups. Usually fairly formal, it is perfect if guests do not have to travel far and will therefore not expect a full meal. If you're holding a tea reception at home, you might want to ask attending friends and neighbors to lend their tea cups for an interesting tea service mixture. Your tea can be catered, or everyone can bring tea sandwiches and cookies.

Offer guests a choice of many delightful teas. Unusual flavors available now include teas of Indian, Chinese, British, and Russian origin, as well as decaffeinated and herbal teas in flavors such as orange spice, black currant, raspberry leaf, and more.

A tea menu can present tea sandwiches and scones with butter, cream, jam, and cookies. Or it can be an elaborate array of foods that makes up a mid-afternoon meal. Sandwiches and sweets should be beautiful and small:

- delicate white bread rounds topped with butter rosettes and decorated with a rose petal
- heart-shaped sandwiches
- tiny croissant sandwiches
- smoked salmon and cucumber on rounds of bread
- breadsticks wrapped in prosciutto, endive, or celery stuffed with Roquefort.
- a huge brioche cut into small sandwiches and tied with pretty ribbons
- side dishes of pickles, tiny black olives, smoked almonds
- roast beef on small rolls; black forest ham on black bread; plus tuna, chicken, or egg salad sandwiches

For dessert, there'll be your wedding cake, of course, but you may want to add some other items, presented on silver trays:

- dainty lemon squares
- heart-shaped cookies
- miniature cheesecake tarts
- sugar-frosted grapes
- strawberries dipped in white chocolate
- petit fours

Champagne for toasting or a nonalcoholic punch ladled from a bowl of ice embedded with flowers should be ready to serve along with the wedding cake. Offer a brut, nonvintage champagne; sweet champagne is optional. Each bottle of champagne contains enough for six to eight glasses, so plan accordingly.

HOW TO MAKE PERFECT ICED TEA

In the summer, offer iced tea as well as hot tea.

Place four teaspoons of tea for each quart of water into a glass jar filled with water. Refrigerate, covered, overnight. Strain out the leaves. For a special serving idea, first moisten the rims of the glasses with a lemon wedge, then dip into sugar. Add the ice and the tea.

For an extra taste treat: Pour hot tea over mint leaves or lemon rind, then refrigerate to chill. Serve with ice, sugar to taste, and sprigs of mint.

Add extra touches to enhance your tea party theme. The first dance? To "Tea for Two," of course! On top of the cake? A tiny Mad Hatter and Alice in Wonderland! Favors? Silvery tea balls (fill them with rice that can be thrown at the bride and groom). Gifts for the bridesmaids? Delicate silver teaspoons, engraved if possible. For decorative centerpieces on the buffet tables, fill a silver teapot with wildflowers.

THE SURPRISE WEDDING

The guests are gathering for a formal luncheon thrown in celebration of a friend's thirty-fifth birthday. As they enter the room, each guest is given a small box wrapped in silver paper and tied with a white satin bow. On each a tag reads "Do not open until the stroke of twelve." Confused but smiling, the guests drink their mimosas, listening to piano music and chatting among themselves about the surprise packages. Cynthia, who has arranged the party for her boyfriend Charlie's birthday, secretly knows all about the mysterious boxes but feigns innocence. Suddenly, at a few minutes before twelve, Charlie, dressed in a tuxedo, interrupts the piano player and takes the microphone. He asks his longtime friend, Cynthia, to join him on the stage. The guests open their packages and at the stroke of twelve read aloud the note inside. The voices of one hundred guests loudly fill the room with a resounding, "Cynthia, will you marry me?" Cynthia, pretending shock, opens her own package, which includes the same message and a beautiful diamond ring. In a moment, she grabs the microphone and asks their gathered friends to help her shout a joyful "Yes!" in response. From somewhere in the crowd comes a minister, ready to perform the ceremony on the spot—before the eyes of the excited and expectant guests. Cynthia and Charlie have been planning this Surprise Wedding for months!

The Surprise Wedding is a new trend for many couples. The bride and groom may both be in on the secret—collaborating to spring their nuptials on family and friends—or one of them may surprise the other with a proposal and ceremony. During the usual toasts, the groom can pop the question to his bride and tie the knot with her before guests have a chance to close their mouths. Couples who have taken part in these Surprise Weddings say that the air of excitement and spontaneity charges the entire event with emotion. Everyone is swept up by the romance. The Surprise Wedding is ideal for second-time brides and grooms who may not want guests to feel that they must bring gifts. (Anyone who wishes to can send a gift later on.) If you are a couple who wants to avoid pre-wedding jitters by keeping the news of the engagement under lock and key, try these imaginative ideas for the surprise of your life:

• Invite guests to what they think is a no-special-occasion party. When guests arrive, they receive a newspaper with headlines that proclaim a wedding is about to take place.

• If the evening starts at your home, offer them a glass of champagne "to travel"—and invite them to step into the waiting cars and limousines (or buses) that will take them to the chapel for the ceremony. Afterward, they'll be spirited off to another mystery location: the reception site, where everything is ready for a fabulous party.

• To make sure guests dress appropriately, announce a formal, black-tie party at an elegant hotel on the pretense of a birthday or job promotion.

• Maintain the element of surprise throughout the evening. Hang piñatas stuffed with favors that blindfolded guests can break open to reveal a shower of surprises.

• Plan a special "surprise dance." Divide male and female guests, then cut a deck of cards in half. Give one set of halves to the women, the other to the men, and watch the fun as they roam the room to find the person with the matching card.

• Toast the guests with, "I guess it's no surprise how we feel about each other."

• Be sure to have a photographer on hand to capture every moment of this spirited adventure.

• Throw everyone off guard by marrying a few days before the planned wedding! One couple changed plans in midstream and married at the bridal shower instead of the wedding. The maids were gathered for a luncheon when in came the men, handing out notes that read, "Roses are red, Violets are blue, Today's the day, The surprise is on you."

• The groom and his guests have been known to join forces and surprise the bride! One groom sent engraved invitations to all the guests, then sent a phony one to his girlfriend, so she would think they were attending *another* couple's wedding. Only when she saw her fiancé standing at the altar, and was handed a bouquet by her daughter, did she realize that this was *her* wedding day—instead of someone else's!

The Legalities

The Surprise Wedding can surprise everyone but the officiant. You will need a marriage license in order for the marriage to be legally recognized. If the two of you are in on the secret together, this won't be a problem. Just be sure to get your blood tests and license in time for the big day. If one of you wants to surprise the other with a wedding, talk your mate into applying for a marriage license— which is to be pocketed and kept handy for "the right moment" (during the valid time period). Once this is accomplished, the Surprise Wedding planning can begin.

THE ALL-NIGHT WEDDING

The sky is like black velvet—with thousands of stars twinkling above. Laughter and music float out of the reception hall doors, which open onto a terrace. Inside, a party is in full swing—confetti blankets the floor, helium balloons cover the ceiling, the band is playing "New York, New York," in honor of the location where the bride and groom first met, and everywhere on the dance floor you can hear the rustle of taffeta skirts. It's almost midnight, but this wedding is set up for nonstop fun. Champagne corks pop as the next song begins; appropriately, the band is playing Lionel Richie's "All Night Long." The excitement has only just begun. Stargazer guides are passed out and a telescope is set up at the east window for everyone to use. This is a night to remember.

Similar to Carnival in Brazil, the All-Night Wedding is a wee-hours extravaganza of nonstop fun that doesn't stop until morning. Beginning at 10:00 P.M. with a seated dinner, and followed by the ceremony (perhaps a stroke-of-midnight exchange of vows on New Year's Eve), the dancing and partying continue until the first rays of sunlight stream through the windows. The cake is cut around 4:00 A.M. Later, as the sun rises, guests are treated to an early-morning wedding breakfast of warm biscuits, fluffy omelets, fresh fruit, hot coffee, and just-squeezed orange juice. In the still-darkened dawn, one bride and groom escaped to a boat docked at the yacht club where their reception was held and motored out for a stunning view of sunrise on the water. What a romantic way to begin a first day as husband and wife! Breakfast was served on board for the couple only.

Dark sunglasses are a thoughtful memento for guests as they leave, to face the bright sunlight. And booking hotel rooms for a long nap is a must now that the sun has risen. (Arrange cab or van service for those who choose to leave and go to bed. No guests should have to drive themselves home after a night of drinking and partying.)

The Logistics

When looking for an All-Night Wedding site, make your intentions absolutely clear to the caterer, musicians, photographer, etc. Since many hotels these days offer round-the-clock services, a hotel ballroom can be the ideal solution. Guest rooms are accessible for those who don't want to stay up all night, yet any guest who retires before dawn can easily rejoin the revelers for the 6:00 A.M. breakfast. Search for the band that will enjoy performing from midnight on, and for a photographer who is an admitted night owl. Flexibility might be called for if someone balks. One professional photographer, for example, might stay until 1:00 A.M. to shoot ceremony and wedding party photographs; a second photographer would arrive to catch the early-morning breakfast shots. (A friend can take some wild candids in between.) If the live band can't stay past a certain hour, switch to a disc jockey and tapes for your favorite dance tunes. Consider, too, hiring a string quartet or pianist to play at breakfast, giving a mellow tone to the party and allowing everyone to wind down.

7.
Helpful Charts and Checklists

Perfect wedding planning requires organization. And organization requires starting early to get all the details of your wedding and reception in order. The more time you have to arrange your affairs, the more relaxed you'll feel about the whole process.

By now, you have found the wedding style that's right for you and your fiancé. Whether you've decided on a Long Weekend Wedding, a Country Wedding, an All-Night Wedding, or a Honeymoon Wedding, they all have many elements in common. How much time you need to plan depends on how complex the wedding will be. Planning a formal wedding can take six months, a year, even two years to secure the perfect site. On the other hand, a private Honeymoon Wedding for just the two of you in Hawaii might take only a couple of days to get off the ground!

Use the following checklists, prepared with your special wedding styles and needs in mind. If your wedding combines elements of two or more wedding styles (a Honeymoon Wedding that progresses to other cities, for example), please draw up your own cohesive checklist using the two separate lists as references. This book is designed to help you keep up-to-date information on reception sites, florists, caterers, bands, transportation, and so forth—so you

can make intelligent decisions and not forget anything.

Along with the checklists, please use the budget-
ing chart to keep track of the various amounts of
money needed for the reception, wedding, and related activities.

THE ULTIMATE WEDDING or THEME WEDDING

At Least Nine Months Before:

——Discuss finances with your parents, including
whether you and your groom plan to pay for some
or all of the wedding expenses. If the groom's parents or other relatives are helping with wedding expenses, they must be included in the discussions as
well.

——Decide whether or not you will engage a wedding consultant.

——Decide on the wedding site.

——Choose a reception site. Explore ideas that suit
your personality or theme: a museum, mansion, or
botanical garden.

——Choose a caterer, according to the guidelines
of the reception site.

——Plan fantasy extras: color scheme, canopies,
fireworks, greenery, candlelight. Make sure your
wedding/reception site will oblige.

——Locate a florist or floral designer.

——Research the best musicians for the reception.

——See a clergy member or judge with your fiancé.

——Choose and order the wedding dress of your
dreams, which carries out your theme.

——Begin a guest list; have your fiancé do the
same.

——Choose your attendants. Let your fiancé know
that he should choose ushers (one for every fifty
guests or so).

——Register for gifts at the stores of your choice.

——Discuss honeymoon plans with fiancé, travel
agent.

Three Months Before:

——Complete guest list.

——Order invitations and start addressing them as soon as they're ready.

——Arrange transportation for wedding party.

——Order wedding rings.

——Select and order attendants' dresses. Confirm delivery date for your dress.

——Hire a photographer for the wedding and reception. If you want a formal portrait taken of yourself before the wedding, hire a portrait photographer now as well.

——Complete honeymoon plans with your groom.

——Iron out details with caterer, florist, organist, etc. Make sure your fantasy extras (such as the release of a hundred helium balloons) are under control.

——Hire the musicians for the reception.

——Schedule doctors' appointments (for blood tests, inoculations, birth control, etc.).

Six–Eight Weeks Before:

——Buy your groom a wedding gift.

——Mail your invitations.

——Have a final dress fitting.

——Have your portrait taken.

——Pick up wedding rings; check engravings.

——Discuss rehearsal dinner with groom.

——Arrange for announcements in newspapers.

——Choose attendants' gifts and guest favors. Match your gifts and favors to the thematic thread that runs throughout your wedding.

——Make sure all necessary documents—legal, medical, and religious—are in order.

Two Weeks Before:

——Get your marriage license.

——Make an appointment with a hairdresser for the big day.

——Check honeymoon reservations; buy luggage.

One Week Before:

———Begin your honeymoon packing.

———Give a final guest count to the caterer.

———Check on final details with the florist, caterer, musicians.

———Work on seating arrangements. Ask your fiancé to let you know of any seating preferences or necessities (divorced family members, disabled guests, etc.).

THE HONEYMOON WEDDING

Seven Months Before:

———Search out locations for your honeymoon wedding.

———Talk with your parents about the wedding budget. It should include the wedding and reception and all that goes with it (flowers, music, transportation). If you will also be hosting other small parties for guests while there, figure in these costs as well. Let your parents know that they will not have to pay for guests to travel to or stay at the site.

———Consult a travel agent for honeymoon wedding ideas.

———Contact the national, state, or local tourist board for information on the destinations that interest you the most. They can send you hotel pamphlets, maps, promotions, information on the sightseeing musts.

Six Months Before:

———Once you've settled on your destination, find out the general rules and regulations for marriage in the location of your choice.

———With the help of a hotel or tourist board, choose a wedding and reception site.

———Settle on the dates of the vacation and the day of the wedding.

———Contact and hire a wedding consultant at the honeymoon wedding site.

———Begin drawing up the guest list; have your fiancé start his too.

———Contact close friends and relatives—in advance

of sending out invitations—to see if they'll be able to join you.

——Locate a clergy member or judge who will be able to marry you there. Confirm with the officiant by phone or letter.

——Choose an attendant or two. Make sure they'll be able to travel on the dates you've chosen.

Four Months Before:

——If necessary, begin the application for a marriage license. Translated documents and long-distance mail take longer to process than documents at home.

Three Months Before:

——Complete your guest list.

——If you're having more than just the immediate family, you may want to send formal invitations. Order invitations and send them out right away; people need plenty of time to plan a trip away from home.

——Book hotels, resorts, or inns early enough to ensure adequate space for everyone at their price ranges.

——Prepare a special Honeymoon Wedding package for all those who will be attending. List dates and times of all the activities planned, plus vital hotel data and other destination information—for example, what the climate will be like, whether passports will be necessary. Remind guests to refill prescriptions and bring any necessary medication.

——Order printed or engraved announcements. You'll want the people who can't be invited or can't attend to hear of your wedding news.

——Order wedding rings.

——Make the final decisions on a caterer, florist, photographer, musicians. Rely on your wedding consultant. Have contracts in hand.

——Make sure your passports are up to date.

——Check on visas.

——Let attendants know what you and your groom plan to wear so that they can dress accordingly. If you'd like them to follow a color theme, let them know now.

Two Months Before:

——Arrange transportation for the group from airport to hotel and from hotel to wedding site or reception site, if it's outside resort grounds.

——Check with your doctor. Get any necessary inoculations if you are traveling to a country where this type of medical precaution would be warranted.

One Month Before:

——Give newspapers wedding announcement information.

——Have final dress fitting.

——Pick up wedding rings; check engraving.

——Review your wardrobe. Make sure you have something appropriate for each activity planned: the Friday-night luau, Saturday-morning brunch, Sunday island tour.

——Dust off your camera. Make sure everything works. Buy film.

——Refill prescriptions that you or your groom may need while there.

Two Weeks Before:

——Check all plane and hotel reservations.

——Send a newsletter to guests with any last-minute information, additions, changes in wedding plans. Include a phone number for guests to call with any questions.

——Buy luggage.

One Week Before:

——Pack for trip.

——Arrange for the wedding dress to be packed separately, possibly insured separately for loss during the flight, if it will be checked as baggage.

——Buy traveler's checks.

——Consult a banker about foreign currency. (Sometimes one gets a better exchange rate in the country itself.)

——Give a final guest count to the caterer.

——Call your wedding consultant to check on final details.

——Call the hotel to check on final details.

——Leave for the wedding destination so you can

arrive a few days before guests and give yourself time to get prepared.

THE LONG WEEKEND WEDDING or SENTIMENTAL JOURNEY

Six Months Before:

——Decide on wedding style: formal, informal. Choose date and time of day you prefer.

——Decide on reception style. Begin planning the surrounding parties to complement, not compete with, your reception. Vary styles.

——Discuss the wedding budget with parents, fiancé, and future in-laws. Will a wedding consultant help with details?

——Call close friends, neighbors, and relatives in the area and talk with them about your Long Weekend Wedding plans. Find out if they can host parties, offer lodging or transportation for guests, and so on.

——Choose a wedding site.

——Decide on a reception site.

——Choose sites for any other parties you plan to give: a tea at an old inn, a piano-bar party.

——Begin drawing up the guest list; have your fiancé start his. Invite from far and wide if you wish; guests will have the whole weekend to enjoy a reunion with old friends and family members.

——Choose attendants. Make sure they'll be able to come for the whole weekend of festivities, possibly even a day earlier than the rest of the guests.

Three Months Before:

——Complete your guest list.

——Order invitations; specify delivery of envelopes first (so you can begin addressing them).

——Print or photocopy informal newsletters announcing the wedding and giving preliminary details of the weekend activities to come. Guests will appreciate knowing about the weekend in advance of receiving the formal invitation. This will enable them to make plans and organize wardrobes.

——Arrange transportation for the wedding party from the wedding to reception site.

———Arrange transportation for guests, many of whom will have no cars of their own. Consider hiring a bus.

———Shop for and order wedding rings.

———Shop for and order attendants' dresses.

———Confirm delivery date of your dress.

———Select a photographer. If you want a photographer for any of the surrounding parties, arrange for this or ask friends to bring cameras.

———Plan reception details with the florist and caterer.

———Make honeymoon plans with your groom. Decide how long you will stay with guests and when you will leave on your honeymoon.

———Scout out lodging for out-of-town guests at nearby hotels and inns. Ask about rates and the amount of advance time needed to make reservations. If possible, reserve a block of rooms, to be confirmed by individual guests. Make lists of neighbors who have offered to put people up and calculate how many guests can be accommodated that way.

One Month Before:

———Plan your getaway. Will you leave by boat during the Sunday-afternoon beach party? Or by antique car after Monday's farewell brunch at a nearby inn?

———Mail formal invitations.

———Mail an updated wedding packet, complete with all weekend activities, host names and numbers, appropriate dress, information on transportation, a phone number for guests to call with any questions.

———Have final dress and headpiece fitting.

———Complete lodging arrangements for out-of-town guests.

———Have a portrait taken.

———Choose gifts for attendants, as well as for those hosting parties in your honor.

———Pick up wedding rings; check engraving.

———Plan a bridesmaids' party.

———Discuss rehearsal dinner plans with your groom and his parents.

———Send announcements to newspapers.

Two Weeks Before:

——Go with your fiancé to get the marriage license.

——Make an appointment with a hairdresser for the wedding day.

——Check honeymoon reservations.

——Ask guests for their arrival and departure information.

——Send an updated Long Weekend Wedding newsletter to guests, including information on which flights will be met by your "hospitality crew" and other pertinent arrival and check-in information.

One Week Before:

——Give a final guest count to the caterer.

——Check on final details with the florist, caterer, musicians, and church.

——Check with hosts of surrounding parties to see if they have any questions or need any help.

——Begin your honeymoon packing.

——Prepare welcome bags or baskets—to be placed in guests' hotel rooms.

THE PROGRESSIVE WEDDING

Six to Nine Months Before:

——Discuss Progressive Wedding ideas with family and close friends from across the country or around the world.

——Set up a tentative itinerary of the cities to which you will travel.

——Contact a travel agent, wedding consultant, and begin to arrange the progression.

——Determine which location will be the site of the actual wedding ceremony.

——Choose wedding and reception sites.

——Plan your color scheme, theme, and any unusual ideas you want to incorporate.

——Ask hosts in other cities to choose their reception sites as well. If asked for your advice, give the host some general ideas, such as "We'd prefer an outdoor celebration."

——Shop for your wedding dress.

——Select and register for gifts. If possible, register

in several cities and wherever wedding parties will be held for you. See if the department store near you has chains in the cities to which you will be traveling.

——Begin drawing up your guest list; have your fiancé start his. Discuss guests lists with hosts of parties in other cities—add to these lists where appropriate.

——Choose attendants for the wedding service.

Three Months Before:
——Complete your guest list for the wedding.

——Make sure guest lists for receptions in other cities are completed as well.

——Order invitations. If you wish, include on or in the invitation a list of the other places where your wedding will be celebrated.

——Order invitations (or make sure hosts have ordered invitations) for the parties leading up to or following your ceremony.

——Arrange your transportation from city to city or country to country. Book hotel rooms where necessary for yourselves.

——Order wedding rings.

——Select attendants' outfits.

——Plan ceremony and reception details.

One Month Before:
——Mail your invitations. Have hosts mail theirs or phone the people they are inviting.

——Have final dress and headpiece fitting.

——Choose your gifts for the attendants and for hosts of other parties you will be attending.

——Go over your Progressive Wedding wear. Decide now what you will need to pack for each part of your trip and what you will wear to each party. Shop for any new outfits. Will your wedding dress be worn again at a second reception? If so, make plans for immediate dry cleaning after the first celebration.

Two Weeks Before:
——Go with your fiancé for the marriage license.
——Buy luggage and check reservations.
——Buy a memory album to begin keeping a scrap-book of your Progressive Wedding.

One Week Before:
——Begin packing.
——Purchase traveler's checks.
——Give a final guest count to your caterer.
——Check on final details with out-of-town hosts.

BUDGETING

You'll need to have a good idea of how much money you can afford to spend on the wedding, receptions, and travel, well in advance. Once you have arrived at a figure, break it down into categories, estimating how much you'd like to spend on each aspect of your wedding—from clothes to food. Use this chart, applicable to all weddings, to keep track of how much you are actually spending. Be sure to fill in the amounts as soon as you know them. Tally costs from time to time to see how close you are getting to the ceiling you originally set. Remember, others will be hosting and financing some of the wedding celebrations.

Ceremony Site Fees, Gratuities _____
Ceremony Accessories; Decorations _____
Candelabra _____

   Huppah _____
   Pew Markers _____
   Aisle Runner _____
   Flowers, Plants _____
   Program _____

Clergy Member _____

Bridal Gown _____
Headpiece _____
Wedding Shoes _____

Accessories (Purse, Stockings, etc.) _____

Going-Away Outfit _____

Dresses/Clothing for any Surrounding Parties _____

Reception Site _____

Caterer _____

Food _____

Wines _____

Champagne _____

Liquor _____

Cake _____

Parking _____

Taxes _____

Waiters'/Bartenders' Gratuities _____

Invitations _____

Postage _____

Printing of Wedding Newsletters _____

Printing of Long Weekend Wedding Program _____

Invitation Extras (Calligraphy, etc.) _____

Wedding Consultant Fee _____

Favors _____

Wedding Party Gifts _____

Gifts for Hosts of Other Parties _____

Bride's Ring _____

Groom's Ring _____

Trip to Wedding Site if Planning Long-Distance
_____

Long-Distance Phone Bill _____

Hotel Accommodations for You/Family for Honeymoon Wedding or Long-Distance Wedding
_____

Long-Distance Travel to Other Cities for Wedding/
  Other Receptions Held in Your Honor _____

Bridal Bouquet _____

Bridesmaids' Bouquets _____

Boutonnieres _____

Corsages _____

Reception Decorations _____

Other Decorations (Balloons, Christmas Trees, etc.)

Photographer _____

Ceremony Music _____
Reception Music _____

Transportation for Bridal Party _____
Transportation for Out-of-Town Guests _____
Chauffeurs' Gratuities _____

Bridesmaids' Luncheon _____
Rehearsal Dinner _____
Wedding Consultant's fee _____

Other Miscellaneous Fees _____

Index

The Adventures of
Balto

The Untold
Story of
Alaska's
Famous
Iditarod
Sled Dog

Patricia Chargot

Since 1978

PO Box 221974 Anchorage, Alaska 99522-1974
www.publicationconsultants.com

ISBN 978-1-59433-042-1

Library of Congress Catalog Card Number: 2006900701

Manufactured in the United States of America.

Dedication

For Per, my sweet Viking.

Acknowledgement

With special thanks to Steve Misencik of the Cleveland Museum of Natural History for his generosity in sharing Balto's story. His enthusiasm sparked mine.

Thanks, too, to Martha Thierry for capturing Balto's essence for the cover of this book.

Contents

Accompanied by his master, Gunnar Kaasen, and Mrs. Kaasen, Balto, the famous Alaska trail dog, on arrival in Seattle, Washington aboard the steamship Alameda, and was given the freedom of the city. Then, he soon left for Mount Rainier to become a motion picture star.
Courtesy of Special Collections, Cleveland University Library.

Introduction

Balto. The great Alaska sled dog has been dead since 1933. But he still stands larger-than-life on Dogdom's Mount Olympus, where the world's great canines are immortalized.

He's up there with Barry, the brave Saint Bernard that rescued mountain travelers buried by avalanches in the Swiss Alps. He shares a golden kennel with Hachiko, Japan's favorite dog, that faithfully searched for his dead master for years outside a Tokyo subway station. His name echoes down the long dog run of history with the brave Newfoundland Tang's, the Earth-orbiting Laika's, the loyal Skye terrier Greyfriars Bobby's.

Yet few people know Balto's true story. Only one small part has been told, and even it has been distorted.

Over the decades, several Balto books have been written. There's even a Balto animated movie, but it, too, is largely fiction. (Balto was NOT part wolf!) Like the books, the movie leaves off where this book begins — and tells the best part of the story.

Balto was only three years old when he helped carry serum across Alaska from Nenana to Nome to save the town's children from diphtheria. As leader of the last dog team in the life-saving relay race, he became an overnight sensation — a BONEa fide international celebrity.

But so much more happened after that. Balto lived for eight more years, experiencing the happy surprises and unexpected sadnesses found in every long life — animal or human.

His days unfolded like a sled expedition to the North Pole, carrying him in an exhilarating rush over smooth snow one minute, an icy hummock the next. And how does the new story end? With a heart-thumping surprise that you can't imagine and neither could have Balto.

So hook up your harness, step into Balto's booties — the little fleece socks sled dogs wear to protect their feet — and mush off to Chapter One.

Whoosh.

Nome about the time of Balto's historic run.
Courtesy of Carrie M. McLain Memorial Museum

Chapter One
Down and Out in a Dime Museum

The dogs' whimpering was too soft to be heard from the street. Outside the old storefront, the party decade was roaring — not just in Los Angeles, but across the country.

It was the wild, jazzy, fun-filled Roaring Twenties. Flappers in short skirts were kicking their legs and twirling the long strands of pearls they wore around their necks. The economy was booming — lots of people were making money and spending it on having fun.

But there was no party going on at the storefront: no jumping, bellowing, yipping. No running, falling, tumbling. No enthusiastic barking — and not one note of joyful husky singing.

The converted store was a "dime museum," a cheap sideshow wedged among gambling dens, illegal drinking dives and other sleazy joints. For 10 cents, visitors — mostly out-of-town businessmen — could ogle an "animal curiosity" — seven famous Alaska sled dogs.

The dogs were Balto, Fox, Alaska Slim, Billy, Sye, Old Moctoc and Tillie, the only female.

Just two years earlier, in February 1925, the team had been heralded as heroes on the front pages of the world's newspapers for saving the children of Nome, Alaska, from a deadly diphtheria epidemic.

In Washington, D.C., the U.S. Senate had suspended official business to listen to stories, poems and songs about the dogs and their young driver, Gunnar Kaasen.

But now it was February 1927. Five of the team's original 12 dogs were gone, and Kaasen had mysteriously disappeared.

The seven remaining dogs were has-beens — even Balto, the bear-like leader with the cute white markings that was known to children across America.

Thousands of families had Balto bookends and used Balto dog food dishes or cat food dishes to feed their pets. But did they think of Balto?

The brave dogs had been forgotten — some would say, shamelessly left to die. Small, hot and windowless, the dime museum was no place for dogs. But it was a nightmare for huskies, which are most comfortable in temperatures of 10 to 20 below zero.

In Nome, the team had lived like other sled dogs — in a huge kennel in the middle of a snow-covered field. The snow was deep and made the dogs want to jump and run. The air was crisp and crystal-clear. It sharpened their already keen senses of taste and smell.

But there was no fresh air in the dime museum, not a ripple of breeze or tiny icebox blast of chill. The stifling conditions were draining the dogs' life force, almost as if some great invisible moose, their dreaded enemy back in Alaska, was slowly stomping them senseless.

After weeks of confinement, the dogs were thin, weak and miserable. Their lustrous fur had dulled, and their once strong pulling muscles had shrunk. One by one, they had sunk into a lethargy, a state between wakefulness and sleeping.

There was no stimulation of any kind, nothing to rouse their spirits. So they lay dreaming of faraway Alaska: of soft, sub-Arctic sunlight, sub-zero temperatures, the tantalizing scents of reindeer, fox and rabbit.

They had come such a long way since the life-saving serum run. Now, they were unable to save their own lives. Tied to their beloved sled in a musty back room of the museum, they wondered: "Is this the end of the trail?"

10

Chapter Two
Back to the Beginning: Balto's Early Life and the Serum Run

Leonhard Seppala (SEP-luh) loved Siberian huskies.

It was 1922, and the friendly, easy-to-train breed hadn't even been introduced yet to the American Kennel Club in New York — let alone officially recognized.

But up in Nome, the little gold town of the far north, Seppala already had raised and bred more Siberians than any other Alaskan musher.

The small but strong Norwegian had been smitten by the small but strong dogs in the early 1900s, when a friend had given him 15 Siberian pups and adult females — all imported from eastern Siberia, a long, watery reach across the Bering Strait from Nome.

Leonhard Seppala with a team of dogs. The dog on the far left is Togo, and the dog on the far right is Fritz. Courtesy of Carrie M. McLain Memorial Museum

But some Siberian huskies were better than others — smarter

and faster, with greater endurance and better dispositions. Like other husky breeders, Sepp — as Seppala's friends called him — felt he could tell "A" dogs from "B" dogs as pups. "A" dogs were used for long-distance runs and races and bred; "B" dogs were neutered and consigned to hauling freight.

Nome had been Seppala's home since 1900, but the frontier outpost had shrunk dramatically since those heady gold rush days. Then, 30,000 residents and visitors clogged the streets. Now, there were only about 1,450 inhabitants fewer people than sled dogs. Still, Nome was a metropolis compared with tiny Skjervoy (ski-YEAH-voy), the Norwegian fishing village where Sepp had spent his boyhood.

Skjervoy had stamped Seppala with a fierceness that rivaled the Alaska winter itself. By any standard, winter was harsh in Nome, 140 miles south of the Arctic Circle. But it was even harsher in Skjervoy, 500 miles north of the Circle, near the Arctic Ocean. And Seppala had felt the full impact of that harshness, like a lion tamer who has seen the inside of a lion's mouth.

Seppala was only 11 when he was first sent to his father Isak's winter fishing grounds. That first winter, he stayed on shore baiting hooks, helping in the cooking galley, scrubbing the mens' clothes and bunking in a small, drafty cabin.

By 14, the young Viking was working aboard his father's beloved boat, the Leviathan — handling the ropes and rigging with raw, reddened hands, hauling up huge nets filled with thousands of squirming cod; sweating one minute, shivering the next.

At night, every bone in his small body ached. He listened to the men tell stories about terrifying sea monsters, and boats and men that had been lost at sea — and felt grateful not to be among them. He returned home to Skjervoy a man, not a boy — with a man's appetite for daring and adventure.

He found both in Nome — first as a gold prospector, then as a sled dog racer. Sepp and his Siberians had won every big race in Alaska, including the 408-mile All-Alaska Sweepstakes three years in a row. He almost always won the "condition prize," too, for finishing the race with dogs that were in better shape than his opponents'. He had a reputation for taking good care of his dogs.

"That man is superhuman," one competitor said of Seppala. "He passed me every day of the race, and I wasn't loafing any. I couldn't see that he drove his dogs. He just clucked to them every now and then, and they would lay into their collars harder than I've ever seen dogs do before.

"Something came out of him and went into those dogs with that clucking. You've heard of some men who hold supernatural control over others? Hypnosis, I guess you call it. I suppose it's just as likely to work on dogs. Seppala certainly has it if anyone has." *

Sepp's No. 1 leader in 1922 — the year Balto was born — was Togo, a nine-year-old gray male with ice-blue eyes, that was small even for a Siberian. Alaska's top husky weighed only 50 pounds! But Togo was "fifty pounds of muscle and fighting heart," as Seppala liked to say. He was a natural born leader that, in Sepp's opinion, had the temperament of genius: Ambitious even as an eight-month-old puppy, he repeatedly broke out of his kennel and followed after Sepp and the big dogs until they finally let him join their team.

On the very day that Sepp hitched him up for the first time — close to the sled so he could keep an eye on him — Togo performed so well that after only a few miles, he was promoted up the line. Soon afterwards, he was made co-leader — alongside old Rusty.

Togo had boundless energy and endurance and an unerring sense of the trail, even in the most blinding of blizzards. Named after Togo Heihachiro, a famous Japanese admiral, he was respected by all the dogs in Sepp's kennel — 32 other noisy, frisky Siberians, including the young Balto.

Balto was one of the lesser huskies, in Sepp's opinion — definitely a member of the "B" team. He was considerably larger than Togo and more ruggedly built, but he was a much slower runner. Sepp had named him for Samuel Johannesen Balto, a famous Sami (SAH-me) and fellow Norwegian who had lived in Alaska for 24 years and had died shortly before Balto was born. (The Sami are an Arctic herding people who live in the northern reaches of Norway, Sweden, Finland and Russia.)

Seppala's boyhood hero had been Fridtjof (FRITCH-uff) Nansen,

*From *The Complete Siberian Husky* by Lorna B. Demidoff and Michael Jennings.

13

the great Norwegian explorer, and Samuel J. Balto had accompanied Nansen on the first crossing of the Greenland Ice Cap. Balto's lively sense of humor had buoyed the moody Nansen's spirits on the long trek across endless snowdrifts and ice floes. But Balto also had been temperamental, complaining and even whining when he felt deprived of some food or exhausted by the grueling journey. Like Nansen, who eventually tired of his Sami guide and declined to invite him on future expeditions, Seppala quickly lost interest in Balto's canine namesake. Unimpressed with what Sepp called the husky's poor work attitude, Seppala neutered him at six months and relegated him permanently to the "B" team.

Still, there was no denying that Balto was cute, with his with long, thick, shiny brownish-black hair, white markings that looked like socks — one short and one long — and button eyes like a bear's. And he had a proud, regal bearing.

He appealed to Gunnar Kaasen, a handsome young Norwegian and newcomer to Alaska who hadn't yet made enough money to buy his own dogs. When he needed a team, he borrowed one from Seppala, who was a mentor to the younger fellow countryman. Kaasen, 21, became the 48-year-old Seppala's assistant. He was a big, rugged man who liked big, rugged dogs. He liked big Balto.

Seppala and Kaasen worked for a large gold mining company, driving dog teams with food and other supplies to the outlying gold camps. In addition to paying Seppala's salary, the company paid for his dog food. It was an important perquisite (PURR-kwi-zit) — "perk" for short, or bonus — because Seppala's real work was training for sled races. Without free dog food, he probably couldn't have kept such a large breeding kennel. His teams also carried sick and injured miners to Nome for medical treatment.

But the serum run was Seppala's most urgent mission yet. When the message went out in January 1925 that children were dying of diphtheria in Nome, Alaskan officials quickly realized that the only way to deliver serum was by dog sled.

Initially, Seppala was to play the major role. As one of the Territory's most skilled drivers, he was asked by Nome officials to set out for Nenana, 674 miles away, to meet the train carrying serum from Anchorage. Nenana was the end of the rail line.

Seppala and his champion dogs were to mush back to Nome. The total trip was 1,348 snow-covered miles!

But officials in Juneau, the Territory's capital, soon came up with a different plan — and a better one. They wired Nome officials to tell Seppala to set off from Nulato, the half-way point between Nenana and Nome. To save time, another musher would carry the serum from Nenana to Nulato.

Then the plan was changed again: Twenty mushers would carry the serum in a relay race. By using fresh teams to cover distances of 18 to 53 miles, the serum was certain to arrive sooner than if two teams each ran more than 300 miles with only brief rest stops. Every minute counted.

But Juneau wired the new changes too late. Seppala had already set off with his best 20 dogs, including Togo. He was out of reach, racing across the wilderness to Nulato.

Before leaving, Seppala had told Kaasen to use the remaining 12 dogs for any hauling that needed to be done while he was gone — with Fox as leader.

But Seppala never made it to Nulato. With 140 miles left to mush, he ran into Henry Ivanoff, another driver, who had just left the village of Shaktolik with the serum. Ivanoff's dogs were fresh, but both men knew that Seppala and his champion dogs probably would make better time to Golovin, 91 bitter miles away. So Ivanoff handed Sepp the serum, and Sepp turned his team around.

Meanwhile, Kaasen was asked to join the relay race. He was to mush to Bluff, 53 miles from Nome, wait for the serum, then carry it 33 miles back to Point Safety, where another musher, Ed Rohn, would be waiting to make the final 20-mile sprint to Nome.

He had no choice but to use Seppala's dogs — and he picked Balto as the leader! Kaasen knew Sepp wouldn't approve, but he felt he was a good judge of dogs, too, and had the right to pick the leader he felt would do the best job. Kaasen felt he saw something in Balto that Sepp had overlooked — a strength, a steadiness of character — qualities that had become apparent only with age and maturity. Balto was a late bloomer!

The team set off. Like an understudy who has at last stepped on stage, Balto rose to the occasion, holding a straight course on the long, windy trip and even saving the team from running into icy water.

Meanwhile, Seppala had decided to take a dangerous shortcut to Golovin across frozen Norton Bay. He knew the ice could break up at any moment and carry the whole team out to sea. But driving around the big bay would add hours to this near-last leg of the serum run. Nome's children were dying. Sepp put his trust in God and set off into the slippery darkness.

At Golovin, Sepp handed the serum to Charles V. Olson, who carried it to Bluff. There Olson handed it to Kaasen, who was waiting for him at a cozy roadhouse. Driver and leader were resting contentedly — Kaasen in front of a wood-burning stove, Balto at his feet, tail thumping. The two clearly had become companions, even friends. They trusted and liked each other. The other dogs were tied up outside.

Nome in the early 1900s. The dark colored dog standing broadside to the photographer is Balto. Courtesy of Carrie M. McLain Memorial Museum.

Kaasen quickly set off for Point Safety, but when he got there, he found his replacement, Ed Rohn, sleeping. Rather than wake Rohn up and wait for him to dress and harness his team, Kaasen decided to make the final dash to Nome himself.

Balto ploughed through snowdrifts and fought high winds for more than three hours in the swirling, crystalline blackness. When the team arrived before dawn, there was no one to greet them — almost the whole town was sleeping.

But relief and elation soon spread through Nome like the golden rays of the dawn itself. The diphtheria epidemic was checked! The children of Nome were saved!

Kaasen and Balto became instant heroes. By daybreak, re-porters and photographers had swarmed the exhausted team, asking questions, wanting details. What kind of dog was Balto? What was his racing record?

A French film crew that happened to be in town asked Kaasen to re-enact his pre-dawn arrival. He obliged, driving the team outside town, then turning around and charging back down Front Street. The citizens of Nome went wild, cheering as if the precious serum were just arriving!

By the time Seppala and Togo showed up, no one was quite as interested in their story, even though their team had traveled 169 miles to pick up the serum and had carried it almost twice as far as any other team — 91 miles! Kaasen's and Balto's team had traveled 53 miles to pick up the serum and had carried it for only 53 miles. But Kaasen and Balto had the spotlight — there was no room in the winner's circle for Seppala and Togo. The contributions of all the other teams were ignored.

Seppala was understandably miffed. For starters, he didn't believe Kaasen's story about not wanting to wake Ed Rohn. He suspected that Kaasen, knowing that news of Nome's plight had captured the world's attention, had simply seen an opportunity and taken it. Why not let Rohn sleep and victori-ously deliver the serum himself? There was no glory in being the second-from-the-last man to carry the serum. Not that this is what went through Kaasen's mind. But it might have been, though he later denied it.

To make matters worse, reporters had mistakenly credited Balto with Togo's accomplishments. Now, Balto was the super Siberian — the veteran racer, skilled navigator, loyal leader that never stopped pulling. The distorted stories had been transmitted around the world. Balto was the toast of New York, London, Tokyo.

But even that wasn't what upset Sepp the most. Togo had run himself to exhaustion on the relay and had badly injured a leg. He would never race again or be able to go on a long run. He would have to retire as Sepp's best leader ever. The sad realization hit Sepp like an icy snowball to the heart. But Balto's celebrity would soon carry him far beyond his simple world into the vast, unimaginable unknown.

Chapter Three
Goodbye, Alaska

Sol Lesser loved making movies.

The young Hollywood producer had gotten his first job in the movie business as a boy, working at his father's nickelodeon, one of the country's first movie theaters. Sol sold ice cream, helped the cashier, operated the projection machine and ushered while the audience — mostly kids — watched short silent films for a nickel — 10 or 12 of them back-to-back: chase scenes, bank robberies, five-alarm fires.

Movies were in Lesser's blood, and the friendly, talkative Californian loved a good story, especially a good adventure story. By 1925, Lesser had made all kinds of short films and one blockbuster — *Oliver Twist*, starring the impish child actor Jackie Coogan — the Macaulay Culkin of his day — and based on the famous Charles Dickens' novel about the adventures of a poor orphan boy in 19th Century London. The full-length film had made a whopping $2 million, enabling Lesser to buy a chain of new theaters that were many times larger than his father's tiny, storefront nickelodeon.

News reports of the serum run immediately inspired Lesser to send a cablegram to Kaasen: Would he be willing to travel with the dogs to make a short educational film? Lesser wanted the team to re-enact the serum run in the majestic, snow-covered Cascade Mountains of Washington state.

But the invitation wasn't Kaasen's to accept. So he gave the message to Seppala, who after all, was the dogs' owner. But Seppala was ambivalent — he had mixed feelings about the offer.

On the one hand, letting Kaasen and the dogs make a movie would make them even more famous than they were already. On the other hand, it would get them out of his sight — at least for awhile. Seppala had kept his disappointment over the serum run to himself, but he had paid a price: It was eating him up inside. He quickly agreed to lease the team to Lesser for 10 weeks for $200, plus traveling expenses. Kaasen would go along as handler.

But the Bering Strait was frozen, and tiny Nome was ice-bound. So Kaasen, his wife, Anna, and the 12-dog team set off by sled for Nenana, a trip that normally took two weeks. But under the terms of Lesser's contract, the dogs had to be delivered in perfect condition — there could be no injuries or deaths along the way. So this time, Kaasen drove the team at a normal pace, stopping for the night at small native villages and taking short, frequent rest stops.

At Nenana, the team caught the train to Anchorage, where they boarded The Alaska Steamship Company's steamship *Alameda* for Seattle. It was Balto's first real adventure! The run to Nenana had been his longest ever — a month-long romp across long stretches of glittering white flatness and up and down mountains. And the boat trip was thrilling! He and the other dogs had never been at sea before or seen whales, walruses, seals, glaciers — though some of them, including Balto, did get seasick. (Don't ask.) That was no fun! But they ate well — fresh salmon stew with rolled oats, rice or cornmeal. And they were petted lavishly by the captain and crew, who treated them like prized pets, not common work dogs. But where were they going? What lay ahead? And would they ever return to Alaska?

Chapter Four
Hello, Seattle!

On March 22, the ship arrived in Seattle, a city of 340,000 people on the sparkling coastal waters of Puget Sound, an eerily deep bay of the Pacific Ocean.

Beneath the sound's deceptively smooth surface, menacing creatures lurked — octopuses with six-foot-long arms, 10-ton killer whales that sent shock waves rolling when they breached.

The city was watery and mysterious, too. So much water surrounded the downtown that it seemed like an island, and in the distance loomed the spectacular, dream-like Cascade Mountains. Balto could see snowy Mt. Rainier, the second-highest peak in North America at 14,410 feet — after Alaska's Mt. McKinley. (Balto had never actually seen Mt. McKinley — it was even farther from Nome than Nenana — but Togo had — once, on Alaska's first big relay race to save the life of a banker.)

The dogs were eager to get grooving, jerking and pulling at their harnesses and jumping all over Kaasen. They were sled dogs, after all, and they wanted to run — to the distant mountains, the only snow they could see anywhere. There was no snow in wet, rainy Seattle.

But when the dogs scampered across the boat's gangplank, they were engulfed by a tidal wave of reporters, photographers and cheering fans — many more than had welcomed them in tiny Nome after the serum run.

Flashbulbs popped. Children chanted: "Balto, Balto, Balto." Kaasen stepped forward, dressed for the occasion in a squirrel fur parka with a wolverine fur hood, wolverine leggings and walrus hide boots. In his sing-songy, Norwegian-accented English, the ruggedly handsome frontiersman shyly answered questions about the serum run. The Boy Scouts showed Kaasen a telegram from their national headquarters instructing them to help the team in any way they could. And Balto was presented with the key to the city — in the shape of a bone!

"For Balto, there was the first sight of a big city, a first ride in an automobile and everywhere hundreds of outstretched hands eager to touch the famous dog," the *Seattle Times* wrote in a story the next day. "He accepted it all with modest dignity becoming to a dog who has acquired such fame."

But the team had work to do. Lesser's film crew was waiting to whisk them to Mt. Rainier National Park, a vast wilderness area about 50 miles southeast of Seattle. The entourage left by truck that very evening — the happy dogs once again barking, yipping and howling as they got closer and closer to snow!

Betty Ann and Shirley Gene Quackenbush on Balto's arrival at Seattle.
Courtesy of Special Collections, Cleveland University Library.

Chapter Five

Back to Alaska, Sort of

Mt. Rainier National Park had been set aside as a national park in 1899. The pristine wonderland was the country's fifth oldest national park — after Yellowstone, Yosemite, General Grant (now part of Kings Canyon) and Sequoia. The huge park was like a chunk of Alaska — one of the best chunks — with old-growth forests, coldly silent glaciers, tremendous snowfields and summer meadows bursting with wildflowers. Small lakes sparkled amid the dense forests like hidden gems — emeralds, sapphires, lapis lazuli, turquoise. The truck made its way to Paradise, in the park's center, where 20 feet of snow blanketed the landscape like a fluffy quilt.

Paradise was one of the snowiest place on earth, with more than 52 feet of snow a year! Guests at the Paradise Inn clomped around on snowshoes and broke trails through the powder on cross-country skis — except on days when there were avalanche warnings.

The huskies were in paradise, all right. The beauty and the silence inspired them to sing the husky songs for which they were so famous — something they hadn't done since leaving Alaska. Their high-pitched voices echoed through the tall Douglas fir trees, which bristled up from the mountain plateau like spears, their branches bent and snow-laden.

For the film crew, shooting the re-enactment of the serum run was hard work. But for the dogs, it was non-stop fun. Kaasen hooked the dogs up to their beloved sled and mushed off into the wilderness. Then he turned the team around and mushed back toward the cameraman, who had his camera rolling.

But sometimes the sky would turn heavy and the sun would disappear, or Kaasen would forget not to look directly at the camera. So the crew had to call for take after take, which was fine with the dogs, who got to run their hearts out — for the first time in weeks!

The were blissed out, completely happy just to be alive and to be huskies. They were happy beyond a gazillion dog bisquits, happy beyond a gazillion pounds of frozen salmon to be back in their familiar world of sun, snow and sub-zero temperatures.

But not for long.

Chapter Six
Balto Goes Hollywood

The dogs had hoped to make the white Washington wilderness their new home. But within days, they were back in gray, rainy Seattle, where they were herded onto another train. Heading south, they soon left the mountain behind them — forever.

The farther south the dogs traveled, the less likely it seemed they would ever see snow again. And train travel was getting old fast. In fact, it was no fun at all. The dogs were separated from one another on the trip, packed up individually in crates set in a stuffy, unrefrigerated cargo car.

In California, the landscape became lush and sweet-smelling, with field after field of orange trees, lemon trees, grapefruit trees, red and green grapes, lettuces, cucumbers and avocados, bright red strawberries and tomatoes. Fields of apricots, melons, olives and asparagus ran together like squares in a patchwork, stretching for 450 miles down a long, wide valley, with towering mountains to the west and east.

California was one big salad bowl! In Alaska, fresh vegetables usually were had only in dreams. There were none in winter, and few in summer — the growing season was extremely short, and people were too busy mining, hunting and fishing to plant gardens.

But this land was something new! California was alive with color — teeming with it, screaming with it — like the ever-changing patterns in a kaleidoscope. Fresh fruits and vegetables could be had year-round, and backyard gardens were little Edens abloom with vines and flowers.

At last, the team arrived in sun-drenched Los Angeles, land of swaying palm trees, golden beaches and glamorous movie stars.

In 1920, Los Angeles had been the country's tenth largest city — but by 1925 it was closing in on fifth place fast, behind New York, Chicago, Philadelphia and Detroit.

The city's young motion picture industry was booming. Each month, more than 10,000 new residents poured into the city of nearly 1 million: actors, writers, directors, publicity agents, movie industry wannabes.

Others were attracted by the near-perfect weather, which was almost always sunny and balmy — sun-kissed, like the state's oranges. Thousands of people from other parts of the country visited Los Angeles on vacation, hoping to see movie stars and their palatial mansions. Los Angeles was a city of dreamers, hopefuls, up-and-comers and success stories.

At 35, Sol Lesser was definitely a success story. The young producer and theater owner knew how to make things happen — how to bring together the many elements needed to make a movie. He could take an idea and make it real, see a movie through from conception to completion.

So Lesser produced an elaborate reception for the team when it arrived in Los Angeles on April 2 — this one even more overwhelming than the one in Seattle. The city's elite turned out and Kaasen and the dogs were treated like dignitaries. Balto was given another "bone to the city," which meant nothing to him, of course. His regular diet was fish; he would have preferred a frozen salmon. He sniffed at the bone politely, then left it.

He didn't have much response to Clara Horton, a glamorous movie star, either, when she placed a collar of white roses around his thickly furred neck.

As for Kaasen, when Miss Horton kissed him, he blushed deeply, saying, "I was never treated like this before."

But everything was unfamiliar, strange. Kaasen and the dogs experienced culture shock, a feeling of confusion and anxiety that can set in when a person — or dog — is first exposed to a culture or environment very different from his or her own. With its large population — almost 700 times the size of Nome's

— movie culture and dry, warm weather, Los Angeles was a double-whammy: It turned their world upside down, like a roller coaster ride on an alien planet.

"It all seems strange here," Kaasen quietly told a reporter in an interview in his suite at the luxurious Biltmore Hotel. "The crowds, the buildings, the traffic — and the climate, it is so different. It's strange to Balto, too, and the other dogs. We must go back north soon."

Dressed in a loose-fitting — and unfashionable — plain black suit, Kaasen looked out of place in the lavish surroundings. Standing by a tall, richly draped window, he looked down fearfully at the busy street eight stories below. "I won't dare to cross the street alone for several days," he mused. "With all those automobiles and streetcars, it is a wonder you don't kill more people than you do. Alaska is safer than this country."

And where was Kaasen's pal Balto? Lesser had put him up in a fancy room at the Biltmore, too! The other dogs were staying in swank kennels on Lesser's Hollywood movie lot, waiting to complete, *Balto's Race to Nome.*

The movie took two more weeks to finish. One day during a break, the dogs were trucked to Third Street Elementary School, where Lesser's son, Bud, 9, and sister, Marjorie, 7, were students.

"It was a nice day — not raining," Bud would recall many years later, when he was in his eighties. "The school went outside to see Balto — about 200 kids. I was so jealous of those dogs getting all the attention — and here I was, lost in the crowd! But walking back to class, I was the hero. Everyone knew the dogs were there because of my father."

The dogs loved being petted by so many pairs of loving, little hands, and Kaasen was gaining confidence in his new environment. But deep down, the whole team felt deeply unsuited to the California lifestyle. Big cities and warm weather were getting old fast — just like train rides — despite all the luxury and attention. They wanted to go home — and they thought they soon would.

Chapter Seven
What Serum Run Is This?

Balto's Race to Nome was only about 20 minutes long, but it was a smash. The whole country wanted to see it. As Lesser said, "Man and dog were fresh from the frozen north and their heroic performance was still fresh in the minds of the nation."

Kaasen and Balto attended the film's premier at one of Lesser's Los Angeles theaters. Then the film was released nationwide, along with a press release so hyperbolic (HIGH-purr-bah-lik), or exaggerated, it would have embarrassed the dogs had they been able to read it!

"It is unnecessary to build up interest in Balto or Kaasen," Lesser assured theater owners in the press release. "It is only necessary to arouse discussion of the fact that you have obtained this picture for your theater. The deed of Balto and Kaasen has gripped the imagination of every thinking adult in America. Now it is within your power to let them see the man, the dogs and the actual saving of Nome re-enacted before their eyes! No more gripping drama has ever been thrown upon the screen than the picturization of the historic exploit of a canine hero!"

The re-enactment "dwarfs fiction," wrote Lesser. In fact, it was fiction. In Lesser's version, Balto not only saved the team from running into ice water on the serum run, he saved Kaasen's life when the driver fell through the ice!

According to Lesser, Balto wasn't Kaasen's first choice as leader — or his second, third or even fourth choice! Balto was promoted to the lead position only after the team encountered a fierce blizzard and the lead dog — unnamed in Lesser's press release — "hesitated, then stopped."

"Kaasen substituted another dog, and he, too, refused to go forward into the wind," Lesser continued. "Two more dogs were tried, but each succumbed to heavy work and stopped.

"Kaasen then took Balto, the shaft dog, from his position next to the sled. Balto was the smallest dog in the outfit. Kaasen could not see the trail 20 feet in front of him. Balto literally dragged the exhausted and dispirited team until they staggered into the streets of Nome."

Hello? What serum run was this? Was Lesser's release based on information from Kaasen? If so, why did Kaasen change his story? Who knows, but does it really matter? No! Balto had performed with great courage — as had all the dogs that participated in the race. But those lucky dogs were back home in Alaska, eating salmon and running around snow-covered dogyards. Balto was stuck in La-La Land, which was no place for huskies.

Chapter Eight
A Song, a Dance, a Dog Act

Lesser had no further use for the dogs, and Seppala didn't particularly want them back. So a theatrical agency booked Kaasen and the team on a long vaudeville tour across North America.

Vaudeville had been the continent's most popular entertainment for decades. It's a French word for a type of fun variety show that featured as many as a dozen live acts: singers, dancers, magicians, comics, unicyclists, clowns, ventriloquists, trained seals and other animal acts. Actors and actresses performed short dramatic sketches and musical comedies; monologists told long stories; poets recited their poems.

Once, Vaudeville theaters had dotted the land from the Rio Grande River to Saskatchewan — across the United States and Canada. Their stages supported thousands of traveling acts, which toured the continent endlessly, attracting large audiences everywhere.

Had it been the 1890s, touring Vaudeville might have been fun for Kaasen and the dogs. They would have met some of the most gifted dancers, singers and clowns that ever graced the world. They would have been part of a generous, large, gypsy-like family with heart and spirit.

But they were not. By 1925, Vaudeville was dying and its great family had dispersed. People were packing new theaters to see movies or staying home to listen to another new form of entertainment — radio, which didn't cost anything beyond the small monthly fee for electricity.

Most Vaudeville theaters had switched to programs offering a combination of live acts and movies — usually only one live act and several short movies. The new film studios and radio production companies had stolen most of Vaudeville's stars.

Kaasen and the dogs spent one-and-a-half years criss-crossing the country by train, stopping at dozens of cities along the way. The dizzied dogs were crated up for days at a time in cargo cars, separated from one another and lonely.

At each theater, Kaasen, now sporting a stylish suit, bow tie and straw hat, politely recounted the story of the serum run and handed out black-and-white studio photos of Balto.

But which story did he tell? The true story? A slightly embellished story? The story in Lesser's press release? No one any longer knows, but whichever story it was, it certainly didn't matter to the dogs. By early July, they were unhappily experiencing the dog days of summer.

Chapter Nine
Balto Becomes an Artist's Model

"Dog days" is a term that refers to the most oppressively hot days of summer, when dogs, especially long-haired huskies — and people — can hardly muster the energy to do anything but lie around feeling miserable. In the northern hemisphere, one of worst places to be at such times is hot, humid New York City, which is exactly where Kaasen and the dogs found themselves in the summer of 1925.

The weather was absolutely stifling, and the frenetic tempo of the city made Los Angeles seem restful. New York City was the center of the American universe: the richest, most powerful, most exciting, most modern city in the world. Since the mid-19th Century, wave after wave of immigrants had pushed the Atlantic port city to its limits. New York had the world's grandest mansions, the tallest skyscrapers, the biggest bridges, the busiest shipping docks, the most modern transportation system. But it also had the world's most crowded neighborhoods, with thousands of poor families stuffed into squalid tenement apartments. In summer, the smell of rotting garbage was overwhelming.

Into this seething cauldron came Balto and the dog team — to appear in theater after theater, none of them air-conditioned. But there was one high point for Balto: He got to pose for a statue for the famous animal sculptor Frederick George Roth at the artist's studio in nearby Englewood, New Jersey.

It would be one of the happiest short chapters in Balto's life. Roth greatly admired all animals and was their true friend.

He had created dozens of beautiful sculptures — a tiger, polar bears, sea lions, elephants, a horse, a little calf straining at its tether and bleating. As one art critic wrote admiringly, Roth was "able to grasp the character of the animals he portrayed." And Roth grasped Balto — his quiet dignity, his keen intelligence, his self-control and patience.

The famous dog and the famous sculptor had a lot in common. Roth, too, had been a late bloomer whose talents were not immediately recognized. Born in Brooklyn, he had wasted precious years as a young man trying to please his father by working in his business. He was unhappy, and failed at it.

Finally, he followed his heart and applied for admission to a respected New York art academy. But the academy director underestimated the self-taught artist — just as Seppala had underestimated Balto. After looking at Roth's sketches, he told him he lacked the talent to become an artist and advised him to find some other line of work.

Roth's belief in himself was badly shaken, but he decided to pursue an art apprenticeship anyway — in Europe. He spent months at zoos in Germany, Austria and Belgium, observing and sketching animals, trying to capture their strength and poise. He also studied animal anatomy and took art classes in Germany, France and Italy.

Finally, Roth returned to the United States to cast his lot in the land of his birth. This time, he was welcomed into the New York academy, where the took yet more art classes. Soon, he began winning important prizes for his animal sculptures — silver medals at major art exhibitions in St. Louis in 1904 and Buenos Aires in 1910; a gold medal at the Panama-Pacific Exhibition in San Francisco in 1915.

By the time Roth met Balto in 1925, he was considered "a master of living animals" throughout the Americas and Europe, as one critic wrote. "The spirit which conceives and touches the objects that have taken shape for our observance is exactly the one you experience in their maker's presence," penned another.

Roth was as kind as he was talented. The 53-year-old sculptor welcomed the travel-weary Balto into his studio as a friend.

He laid out tasty dog treats and a bowl of cool water, which he kept filled as the weather was unrelentingly stifling and there was no air conditioning yet in America.

Roth was deeply impressed by Balto's self-composure — his ability to sit quietly for hours while the artist observed him and made sketches. Balto seemed to understand Roth's gentle commands, trying his best not to move a muscle — except for his tongue, of course. It was so hot, he couldn't stop panting. Dog spittle flew all over Roth's couch, but the artist didn't care. It was a small price to pay for the privilege of getting to know and draw such a noble animal. When a *New York Times* reporter visited, Roth praised Balto lavishly as a good artist's model. His comments appeared in a story in the paper.

But Balto's career as an artist's model was short-lived. He and the team soon boarded another train bound for yet another faraway city and another Vaudeville theater — and another and another. Life on the road became a blur of strangers, strange places and even stranger events.

In December, they appeared with Santa Claus in Kansas City, Kansas, where some of the dogs were sold to the building superintendent of the *Kansas City Star*, the city's newspaper. The other dogs were crated up and sent by train back to New York City, where a publicity agent arranged for them to visit an animal shelter — of all places! (This was somewhat ironic, or darkly humorous, as the crates that Balto and the team traveled in on their many long train trips were a lot like the tiny kennels at the shelter filled with unwanted dogs and cats. Which dogs were worse off — the famous team or the unknown strays?)

On December 16, Balto and Kaasen attended the unveiling of Roth's statue in New York's Central Park. It was the city's first statue commemorating a dog, and about 100 people turned out for the ceremony.

The striking bronze statue was larger-than-life and set atop a large granite rock on the east side of the elegant park near 66th Street. From the rock, the huge dog surveyed the distance — as if he were searching for a trail in a blinding snowstorm. Roth had portrayed Balto panting heavily — perhaps imagining he had just run many exhausting miles to deliver serum. The dog's great bronze legs were spread apart; the noble body leaned forward powerfully; the gaze was intense and intelligent. Even the fur seemed life-like.

Balto could not have cared less. He had no response at all to the statue, though he was happy to see Roth again. And his massive neck snapped around when he sniffed other huskies — two showed up on leashes with their owners. But the New Yorkers and Kaasen kept the dogs apart.

Ho-hum. By Christmas, the dogs were in Toronto for an appearance at yet another Vaudeville theater. Would they ever find a home?

Chapter Ten
Seppala and Togo Show Up

In the summer of 1926, Seppala was invited to visit New England. The sport of sled dog racing, which had started in Nome, had spread to several northeastern states, and Sepp wanted to get in on the action. And he had a 10-day contract to drive his dog team around the ice arena at Madison Square Garden in New York City. Togo was to receive a gold medal at the Garden for his part in the serum run — better late than never!

So Sepp set off by steamship with sleds, racing equipment and 44 dogs. It was a wild, chaotic trip. Also aboard was a team of 12 Malamutes — the native dogs of Alaska — and their driver, as well as some Eskimos and their reindeer. By the time the ship reached a whaling station in the Aleutians, the long island-necklace in the Bering Sea, the captain was about ready to toss all the dogs and both owners overboard. The Malamutes were great howlers, and every time they started howling their Siberian husky shipmates would join the chorus. The sound was unbearable, and there was no escape from it.

The seas were choppy and there was much seasickness among men, dogs and reindeer. They couldn't get off the ship fast enough when it made a brief stop at a whaling station on Kodiak Island, known for its large population of Kodiak bears. Sepp bought 16 pounds of fresh whale meat, and the dogs feasted. But the trip continued to be rough, and four pups died between Kodiak and Seattle.

In Seattle, there was more bad news: The agents who had arranged Sepp's tour and were to pay for his expenses had gone out of business. Sepp and the dogs were on their own, with hardly any money and no place to stay. But not for long. Seattle had a large Norwegian community, and a fellow countryman offered to put Sepp and the dogs up — Sepp in his home, the dogs in a horse barn.

And the agents came through with an eight-day contract to show the dogs in Bellingham, Washington — for $1,500, a whopping sum back then — about $14,500 in today's dollars. The city wanted the famous musher to drive the team down main street — on hard pavement!

The team was soon traveling across the country by train — to Kansas City, Kansas, for 10 days, where Sepp and the dogs paraded through the streets and appeared at a ball park and a livestock show; to Dayton, Ohio, where they appeared at the city's largest department store and attended a banquet held in their honor. From Dayton, the team visited 50 small Ohio towns — in a truck decorated to look like an Eskimo igloo! They were a big hit. At each stop, Sepp gave a short talk in the town square on the serum run and life in Alaska.

The team's popularity seemed to precede them from town to town, growing and picking up momentum like a snowball rolling downhill. In some towns, the crowds were so large the police had to be called in to prevent the dogs from being trampled.

Everywhere they went, Sepp and the dogs made friends and had fun — in Grand Rapids, Michigan, where they appeared at another department store; in Detroit, where they staged a short race on Belle Isle, the city's emerald green island park; in Providence, Rhode Island, where one of the younger dogs almost met disaster when he accidentally jumped off the roof of a five-story building. Fortunately, he landed unharmed on a fire escape one story below.

But the stops were a mere prelude. The real reason Sepp had made the long, dangerous trip was to appear at Madison Square Garden — and not merely to drive the team around the ice arena between hockey games.

Togo was to be formally decorated in a special ceremony for his part in the serum run. The world's greatest sled dog was to receive a gold medal from Roald Amundsen, the world's greatest living explorer — before a crowd of 20,000 people. Sepp would be vindicated (VIN-dih-kay-ted), or set free from the wrongs that had been committed against him. The hurt and anger that had tormented him for so many months would be buried forever under an avalanche of adoration. Balto's role in the serum run would be forgotten. It was little Togo that America would remember.

Chapter Eleven

Kaasen, Go Home!

Roald (ROW-ahld) Amundsen was one tough dog biscuit. Like all Norwegians, as a boy, he had read stories about the ancient Viking explorers. Like many of them, he had imagined himself as a Viking, standing at the prow of a ship with both ends curved upwards and a sea serpent for a figurehead.

But Amundsen took the fantasy further. At age 14, he decided to become an Arctic explorer when he grew up and secretly started to train for his first expedition. To toughen himself for the perils of polar travel, he would leave his bedroom windows wide open on winter nights — against his mother's wishes. While she slept, he would stand in front of the windows and expose his bare chest to the fierce Arctic winds whipping through the silent streets of Oslo, the Norwegian capital.

The young Amundsen also began eating his own leather boots and bones salvaged from the kitchen garbage! His hero, the great British explorer Sir John Franklin, had once survived for three weeks on such rations on an unsuccessful attempt to zigzag across the top of the world in a ship. Amundsen wanted to see whether he could survive on the same hard-to-chew fare — in case he, too, someday faced starvation on his own search for a Northwest Passage.

In 1905, when he was just 33, Amundsen did discover a navigable passage between the northern Atlantic and Pacific oceans — in his ship, the Gjoa. He and his men did suffer from hunger on the long journey, though they didn't have to eat bones or their boots! Amundsen also was the first explorer to reach the South Pole — in 1911 by dog sled, though most of his dogs died on the trip. (Don't ask.)

So when Amundsen visited the United States in 1927, he was a living legend, a modern-day Viking revered everywhere he went. He was also a commanding presence, even an intimidating one. Years of polar hardship had weathered his massive face into a blob-like, leathery terrain of deep crevices and pocked hollows. He looked at least 30 years older than his actual age — 55 — but then he had looked 66 when he was 33!

But behind the severe exterior was a warm, wise and caring human being. Amundsen had been well-liked — even loved — by the many men who had followed him on expeditions. They felt he understood and respected their thoughts and feelings. And Amundsen had an uncanny ability to anticipate their needs — to know when they needed to rest, eat, get going, mourn, celebrate.

Amundsen also knew what it felt like to be upstaged. In 1926, he and a young American, Lincoln Ellsworth, had led an air expedition from northern Europe over the North Pole and west to Alaska. When the airship landed, Amundsen and Ellsworth left for Nome to telegraph their feat to the world. But their brash Italian navigator, Umberto Nobile, beat them to it — by ordering the airship's radio operator to tell Nome — and the world — that it as he who had triumphed. Nobile soon joined the two expedition leaders in Nome, and the three men traveled to Seattle, where Nobile appeared in his spiffy Italian army union. He was swarmed by the press, stealing the spotlight from the expedition's real leaders, Amundsen and Ellsworth, who were dressed in heavy winter clothes. He looked like a celebrity; they looked like everyone else from Nome — common frontiersmen.

Nobile later traveled across the country on a lecture tour, claiming credit for the air expedition everywhere he went. The tour was so successful, in fact, that it almost capsized Amundsen's plans for a similar tour.

So Amundsen knew how Seppala probably was feeling on the eve of his Madison Square Garden appearance: He was worried that Kaasen and Balto somehow would again steal his and Togo's spotlight.

Amundsen and Seppala had been good friends for more than 15 years — since Amundsen's first visit to Nome to buy sled dogs for an expedition to the North Pole. He bought a team of Seppala's Siberian huskies, including Togo's father, Suggen. But the expedition was scrapped when Admiral Robert E. Peary reached the Pole first in 1909. Seppala agreed to take the dogs back, and the two men remained friends.

Now, it was December 1926 and the two friends were about to meet again. Amundsen was in Chicago, where he had just given another lecture. By coincidence, Kaasen and Balto were in Chicago, too, appearing at yet another Vaudeville theater!

Amundsen was set to board a train for New York, where he was to present Togo with his medal. On his way to the station, he stopped by the theater and followed Kaasen backstage after the show. The much younger Kaasen was understandably awed by his much more famous fellow countryman and listened carefully to what he had to say.

Amundsen gently but firmly told Kaasen to go home to Nome, that it was time to get out of Seppala's way. Kaasen left the next morning, stranding the dogs and bringing the Vaudeville tour to a screeching halt.

Chapter Twelve
Does Anyone Want
Seven Brave Dogs?

With Kaasen gone, the dogs had no one to tell their story. With no story, our heroic huskies were, well, just seven cute but mute dogs. The theatrical agency that had booked them on their long Vaudeville tour was miffed. As far as it was concerned, it now had no act. The dogs didn't do any tricks, after all. And so many people already had seen them that their fame had dimmed; audiences wanted something new.

Who owned the dogs? Was it Seppala? Was it the theatrical agency? Was it Kaasen, who could have bought the dogs from Seppala with money from his earnings as a Vaudeville presenter? Was it Lesser, as one book on Seppala, written in 1930, claims? Lesser's son, Bud, who was alive when this book was written, insisted his father never owned the dogs. We may never know. What is known is that at some point after Kaasen left for Nome, the dogs were sold to a man named Sam Houston and ended up in a Los Angeles dime museum, one of the lowest forms of entertainment in the United States at that time — or ever.

Chapter Thirteen
The End of the Trail

By the 1920s, dime museums were no longer a dime a dozen in the United States. Like Vaudeville, their day was over. But unlike Vaudeville, whose passing is still lamented, the death of dime museums today is considered a good thing.

Most dime museums were "freak shows," a term for cruel exhibits that featured people with physical deformities or abnormalities: women with beards or terrible skin disorders; men with excessive hair on their faces and bodies; people who were extremely short or tall; very, very fat people; people so skinny they looked like human skeletons; Siamese twins, or two people joined together at birth; albinos, or people whose hair and skin were milky white because they lacked the pigment that creates color; people with extra limbs or no arms or legs at all; even children with humps on their backs who couldn't stand and had to crawl.

Such "human oddities," as they were shamefully advertised, were given names like "elephant girl," "green alligator boy," "the human ostrich" and "half man-half monkey."

Today, it's hard to imagine that dime museums ever existed — or that Balto, Fox, Alaska Slim, Billy, Sye, Old Moctoc and Tillie could have ended up in one. But they did — unbeknownst to their millions of fans around the world.

The faithful dogs had done nothing but help humans in every way they could. They had helped Kaasen carry serum to Nome, helped save the lives of the city's children, helped Lesser make a movie, helped countless Vaudeville theater owners make money, helped Roth create a prize-winning statue. In every case, they had done their best, putting their big husky hearts into the job at hand.

Now, they were being discarded like so many rusted out sleds. What else are we to think about the sad conditions in which the dogs now found themselves?

The dime museum had seen happier days, too. Like many such "museums" in the 1920s, it had once been a nickelodeon, one of the country's first movie theaters. (Lesser, you may recall, had worked in his father's nickelodeon as a boy.)

"Nickelodeon Madness" swept the country in 1905, when thousands of the tiny theaters opened. They were mostly converted stores, with only 50 to 100 plain wooden chairs. Short films — each only a few minutes long — were projected onto a sheet of white canvas. The stories were simple and action-oriented: chase scenes, bank robberies, three-alarm fires, boxing matches.

Kids loved nickelodeons, though some adults spoke out against them, saying they taught boys how to be bandits and girls how to kiss! The theaters were open from 10 a.m. to midnight, with three or four films running continuously with short intermissions. For a nickel, you could stay as long as you liked, cheering for the good guys, booing the bad guys and shouting made-up dialogue with your friends.

It was okay to talk and make noise because the films were silent — you couldn't hear the actors speak because the technology hadn't yet been invented. So the nickelodeons were like parties, sometimes with ice cream and peanuts. At intermission, the audience sang songs like *Take Me Out to the Ball Game*. Some nickelodeons had piano players or player pianos, mechanical devices that played themselves as if they were being played by ghosts.

But by 1915, "Nickel Madness" was over. The nickelodeons disappeared almost as quickly as they had opened. Small and poorly ventilated, they were driven out of business by bigger theaters that showed longer, more interesting silent films.

By 1927, the Los Angeles dime museum that had featured the famous dogs from the serum run was a mere ghost of its former fun-filled self. It was impossible to imagine children's laughter or anyone having a good time in the place, let alone seven Siberian huskies with thick fur and a craving for fresh air and freezing temperatures.

The dogs were visibly suffering — panting non-stop, which is how dogs sweat, and drifting in and out of dark dreams. If dogs feel the same emotions we do — as some scientists now believe — every member of the once-happy dog team was listlessly depressed. And as the team's leader, Balto was the most depressed of all. Would they ever be able to run and play again? Would they ever get out of this forlorn place?

They were not the first brave huskies to give their all to humans only to be discarded. Seppala's boyhood hero, Fridtjof Nansen, had used 30 huskies to haul supplies on his grueling but unsuccessful attempt to reach the North Pole — and killed them one by one for dog food.

"We wear our dogs to shreds, like articles of clothing," Hjalmar Johansen, Nansen's companion on the journey, wrote in his diary. Nansen and Johansen had to shoot the last two huskies, Thug and Caiaphas, near the end of their trip when they set out in kayaks to finally reach land. The dogs' additional weight might have toppled the craft, and leaving them behind would have sentenced them to an even crueler fate — starvation.

Amundsen, too, had used huskies to win the South Pole. But of 52 dogs, only 18 survived the trip. After estimating how much food each man and dog would need, Amundsen decided it was too much, that hauling so much food would slow down the dogs, which could threaten the trip's success and even the lives of his men. To lighten the load, Amundsen changed his nutrition plan: Some of the dogs would be eaten — as dog food and food for the men. When Amundsen later was criticized by animal rights groups, he said, simply: "You slaughter beef cattle for food. We used dogs."

Balto hadn't been eaten, but he and the other dogs had been used — and discarded. Who would not agree?

Balto lay his head on his snow-white paws. Overcome by a sadness deeper than the deepest snowdrift, he sank into a paralysis of uncaring — about either himself or the other dogs. Following Balto's lead, as always, Fox, Alaska Slim, Billy, Sye,

Old Moctoc and Tillie soon sank into the terrible emotional quicksand, too.

The dogs drifted into a no-dog's-land of near-wakefulness, not-quite-sleeping. It was torpor, a state of semi-hibernation. But unlike animals that are meant to hibernate — and dogs are not — the huskies were not conserving energy and consuming their own body fat to get them through winter. Their life-force — their very will to live — was draining away. It was their darkest hour, the point at which living becomes dying if no medicine or miracle intervenes. The dogs were so beaten down that they barely looked up when a man walked into the dime museum.

Chapter Fourteen
The Rescue

George Kimble had a heart as big as Antarctica. Short and bald, the Cleveland businessman had been a boxer in his youth in Brooklyn, New York. Boxing — and life in the working-class borough across the bridge from upscale Manhattan — had made him tough and street-smart. But it was his big heart that had made him a success.

Kimble was a sheet metal contractor. He traveled around the country selling tons of metal sheets to factories to build things like cars, appliances and shelving. He was good at it because he knew his market and because he liked people. He liked to meet new people; he had a good time visiting with them in their offices and taking them out to lunch.

Kimble liked animals, too. He never walked by a dog without stooping to pet it and whisper a few kind words. He treated all living things with respect, even when he was angry or frustrated. And Kimble was plenty angry when he chanced upon the dime museum one afternoon in February, 1927. He was in Los Angeles on business and happened to be walking through the city's seedy entertainment district.

Looking up, he saw the word "MUSEUM" plastered in letters so big he could have read them from a block away. Underneath "MUSEUM," were crude, hand-lettered signs that read: "Big Act," "All Alive!" But it was a small black-and-white photograph in the dirty window that caught Kimble's eye.

The portrait was of a hero as familiar to most Americans as would be Charles Lindbergh, the dashing young aviator who would soon make the first nonstop solo crossing of the Atlantic in his monoplane, *The Spirit of St. Louis.*

It was Balto! Kimble stopped with a jolt. He studied the museum's short handout: "Last Chance to See the Great Balto and His World-Famous Alaska Huskies, Undoubtedly the Bravest Dogs That Ever Lived."

Kimble was incredulous (in-KREj-yew-luss) — unwilling to believe the claim was true. How could Balto possibly have become an exhibit in a cheap sideshow? Was it some sort of gimmick, or trick, to get people to spend a dime? Frowning sternly at the ticket-taker, he paid his dime and stepped through the darkened door.

What Kimble saw in the museum's hot, airless back room appalled him. Adrenalin surged through his body like an electrical charge, just as in the old days, when he would step inside the boxing ring. But he didn't want to hit anybody. He simply wanted to help the scrawny, whimpering dogs. And he saw instantly that it wasn't going to be enough to pet them and fill their empty water bowls. He had to get them out of there — as soon as possible. In a flash of inspiration, he knew exactly how.

Chapter Fifteen

Read All About It!

Kimble, who was well-known in Cleveland's business community, immediately sent a dispatch to an editor at the *Cleveland Plain Dealer*. In the telegram, he described the dogs' plight and asked the paper to help him launch a campaign to raise money to buy the dogs from whoever owned them.

"It was some kind of shame that those heroic dogs — who had saved a city — should end their days in a dusty dime museum," Kimble wrote, ending: "Shame on mankind." The paper responded quickly — as good newspapers should in times of crisis. Within hours, it authorized Kimble to negotiate the deal. Once the owner agreed to sell the dogs, the paper would launch a campaign to raise the money.

The next day, February 21, the *Cleveland Plain Dealer* printed a short story about the dogs' plight. Kimble was good at making deals and soon made one with Sam Houston, who agreed to sell the seven dogs for $2,000, which was a lot of money in those days — $19,420 in today's dollars. But there was one major sticking point: The money had to be raised in 10 days, or the deal was off.

A Cleveland Balto Committee of prominent citizens was formed, and on March 1, the *Plain Dealer* ran a story announcing the campaign to raise money to buy the dogs. Within 24 hours, more than $200 was raised.

That news was reported on March 2 in a story listing the name of every person who had contributed, along with the amount he or she had given.

The Western Reserve Kennel Club had given $50 — $485.50 in today's dollars! Kimble had given $25; several people had given $1, and one person had given 50 cents — for a total of $205.50.

The city's response was explosive. People from every segment of society responded — adults as well as children, rich people as well as poor, each giving what he or she could, sometimes quarters, nickels or even pennies.

To keep the campaign alive, the *Plain Dealer* wrote daily stories about the citizens' generosity and continued to list the names of every contributor and contribution. "CHILDREN CHIP IN TO SWELL BALTO FUND; Contributions Reach $338 as Invalids, Workers and Institutions Get Behind the Campaign," the headline on the March 3 story heralded. The story began, "Balto's fund took another leap toward its goal of $2,000 yesterday as children, invalids and employes of several companies, and workers in offices, public libraries, banks and the Museum of Natural History got behind the movement." ("Invalids," a term rarely used today, meant people in nursing homes and sanatoriums, or places where sick people went to rest and recuperate.) Some kids chipped in their lunch money or the money they would have spent on candy.

Three Cleveland radio stations helped out by broadcasting appeals for contributions. Radio stations in New York and Detroit broadcast appeals, too. Theaters donated a percentage of their box office receipts or put collection boxes in their lobbies; restaurants set special "Balto" cans on their counters. Three glamorous young models, wrapped in raccoon coats and wearing cloches, or cute little close-fitting hats, sailed through the streets in an open convertible, even though it was cold out, holding a sign that boasted: "Watch the *Cleveland Plain Dealer* Bring Balto to Cleveland."

Every day, there was a new story with a new total for the amount of money raised. Then on Tuesday, March 8, the campaign hit a potentially serious snag: The paper announced that another group, the Los Angeles Alaskan Society, had told Houston it was prepared to buy the dogs if Cleveland failed to meet its 10-day deadline. "WEST EAGER TO BUY BALTO BEFORE CITY" the *Plain Dealer* warned. "Los Angeles Society Set to Make Purchase; Option Expires Tomorrow; Don't Fail at $1,382!"

Roald Amundsen, who was to speak in Cleveland on Friday, had sent a telegraph to the paper the previous day in support of the campaign, and his statement was included in the March 8 story: "Do what you can for these brave dogs and secure them a bright future. They certainly deserve it."

The *Plain Dealer's* March 9 story was even more ominous: "BALTO MUST HAVE $500 BY TONIGHT." It ran on the front page with a large photograph of five of the dogs, including Balto, and five children — Clevelanders and former Clevelanders who were in Los Angeles and had visited the dogs. The plea and picture sparked a last-minute spurt of generosity, pushing the fund over the top.

The next morning, the fund hit $2,245.88 — more than enough to buy the dogs. "CITY WINS BALTO BY GOOD MARGIN; Huskies to be Shipped at Once," the day's headlines proudly proclaimed.

In a short interview, Amundsen, who had arrived in Cleveland, commended the city for its humanitarianism. The City of Oslo, Norway, had once done for another dog what Cleveland was doing for Balto, he said. The dog had accompanied him on his historic expedition to the South Pole — and was the only husky of 100 to return. (Does the story sound familiar? It should.) Amundsen said that when he returned home, Oslo voted to let the dog roam freely around the city for the rest of its life, as a kind of canine honorary citizen. Butcher shops agreed to give the dog free meals. When it died — its name wasn't given in the story — taxidermists preserved the corpse, which Amundsen said was in an Oslo museum. (And what about the other 99 dogs — or 53 dogs, depending on whose version of the expedition you read — that failed to return from the trip? The story didn't say, but we already know, don't we? They were eaten!) Elation swept through Cleveland, filling everyone with pride — as if the Cleveland Indians had won the World Series. The 1,200 people who had given money — and even those who hadn't — felt really good about what their city had accomplished in record time. It was as if everyone had gotten report cards with all "As" — As for Altruism, or do-goodism. The final tally was $2,362.94 — enough to pay for first-class shipping for what would be the dogs' last, but best, train ride across the country.

Chapter Sixteen
All Aboard the Balto Express

Balto, Fox, Alaska Slim, Billy, Sye, Old Moctoc and Tillie emerged from the dime museum into the soft California sunlight. As weakened as they were, they felt hopeful and happy — as if the long Arctic winter had just ended and the sun had just popped over the horizon after months and months of darkness. They stopped whimpering, and their hearts began to sing again. The strongest among them even sang a few trial notes of the happy song for which huskies are so famous.

Kimble had arranged for the dogs to be trucked to a ranch outside the city to rest up for their long train ride home. Home? At last, they became part of the lush California landscape, with its fertile valleys, faraway mountains and sweet scent of ripening oranges. It was like a trip to a spa!

After weeks without sunshine, fresh air or human warmth, the dogs got to run again and were showered with attention and affection. They were bathed and professionally groomed. They dined al fresco, or outside in the open air. They ate fish laced with ground up pills with all the nutrients they had been deprived of for so long. Their fur began to regain its beautiful luster. Balto's white "socks" looked freshly laundered; his dark brown fur gleamed like sable. The dogs looked — and smelled — like great, regal Siberians again — awesomely handsome (except for Tillie, the only female, who was awesomely beautiful).

Finally, the dogs were crated up individually and sent with their sled and harnesses in a cargo car of a train bound for Cleveland. But these crates were like roomy, first-class kennels, little relaxation tanks where the dogs could float in a waterless sea of comfort. And the cargo car was posh: Owned by the American Railway Express Company, it was filled with gold and silver bullion, or gleaming bars that had not yet been minted into coins, and fresh flowers — a trove worthy of Tutankhamen, the ancient Egyptian pharaoh buried in a vault of gold!

The cross-country trip took three days and seven hours, with many stops along the way. Each day at 6 p.m., Mr. G. M. Watson, a Balto Committee member and American Express official, tapped into his national telegraph wire and interviewed the train's baggage agent — in Santa Fe, Denver, St. Louis. "How are the dogs doing?" he would ask. "What did they eat for dinner?" He would take notes and relay the information to the *Plain Dealer*. The dogs' cargo car was dubbed the "The Balto Pullman," a reference to the famous Pullman passenger car, which had especially comfortable furnishings. Excitement mounted as the train rolled closer and closer to Cleveland.

Chapter 17 Seventeen
The Dogs Become Zoomates

The dogs started barking as soon as the train pulled into Cleveland at 9 a.m. on Wednesday, March 16. They were quickly uncrated, put on leashes and led off the train. But there was no repeat of the long-ago scene in Seattle, when the team was engulfed by fans, reporters and photographers. This time, there was no official welcome, no blinding cameras, no smothering fans. Train-lagged and stiff from their 79-hour trip, the dogs would soon get what they most needed: a good stretch and a good meal.

A city truck whisked them away to the Brookside Zoo, where they were taken to the basement of a large building that housed lions, tigers and parrots. To the exotic din of roar and squawk, the dogs were fed all-they-could-eat servings of boiled beef, dog biscuits and milk. They ate quickly, then went to bed — gladly — behind a wire screen inside the kennel-sized crates from the train.

For the next two days, the dogs rested, ate and played in the building's basement and outdoors. A team of veterinarians examined them all, pronouncing each to be in "reasonably good health," the *Plain Dealer* reported. Each day, the dogs were escorted outside and allowed to run around the zoo grounds. They were petted lavishly by the kindly zoo staff and — yes! — their little paws were lovingly massaged, just as in the old days in Alaska, when Kaasen would sometimes rub them energetically to remove the ice after an especially hard run. But these massages were more gentle — more sensual, or luxurious.

They made the dogs tingle and want to roll around! Everyone was so nice!

After so much suffering and sadness, the dogs began to come alive again, one by one, like a sleeping princess and six sleeping princes awakening from a spell. The life that had drained out of them in the dime museum began to flow back, filling them with renewed vigor, spirit and Siberian husky-ness! They would soon be their old selves again. But would the good time last?

Chapter Eighteen
Cleveland Celebrates "Balto Day"

On Saturday, the zoo staff mounted the team's long wooden sled on a dolly, or platform with wheels. The dogs were to pull the sled through the city's streets in a big parade at 1:30 p.m., but there was no snow. Hopefully, the wheels would glide over cobblestones and streetcar tracks as smoothly as iron runners over snow!

All morning, a light drizzle fell on the elegant Lake Erie port city. But the enthusiasm of the dogs' many well-wishers was undampened. By 1 p.m., thousands of fans lined the downtown parade route, standing six and eight deep at every curb. Thousands more hung their heads out of high office windows to glimpse the famous dogs — and to soak up the good feeling that flooded the city like Erie overrunning its banks.

At 1:30 p.m., the parade left Frankfort Avenue at Sixth Street for the long march to City Hall. Four mounted police officers, dressed in bright yellow rain slickers, led, followed by a dozen more police officers on motorcycles. The members of the Balto Committee rode by in 15 Buick sedans, followed by more police on motorcycles.

Next came Costello's 12-piece band, which everyone knew because it had played at Indians' opening games for years. The musicians roused the crowd with their brass instruments. A troop of bright-faced Boy Scouts shyly carried a 10-foot-by-12-foot map of Alaska, showing the exact route of the serum run. Then came the dolly, pulled by Balto and his six teammates looking more regal and brave than ever!

Balto held his head high, carrying himself with the natural dignity of a true leader. (The next day, a reporter would describe him in the paper as having a "fox-like keenness, with ears that are always alert.") Even Old Moctoc, the oldest dog, rallied, caught up in the fun ride and cheering. With his sharp features and coarse coat, some people thought he was a wolf!

A zoo attendant with a long leash walked alongside each dog — just in case, though the dogs were harnessed to the sled. To make the sled-float seem authentic, the zoo staff had rigged it for the North, with a 300-pound pretend load lashed under a bearskin. There was even a pretend package of diphtheria serum — a small box wrapped in fur to keep the "serum" from freezing.

"The Nightingale of Alaska," Miss Marye P. Berne, a cabaret singer who was brought up in the Alaska Klondike, stood in for the missing Kaasen as driver. Dressed in her old fur parka and hood, fur boots and fur gloves, the former musher rode the 12-foot sled's brake — a large iron claw under the platform — to slow Balto down when things got rolling too fast. And they did — about every other block.

Five "sourdoughs," or old Alaska hands, who lived in Cleveland, escorted the team to prevent mishaps. Fortunately, they were able to stop the dogs in the nick of time each time they threatened to knock the Boy Scouts onto the sidewalk or run into the band member's heels.

The hour-long parade wound its way in stops and starts through the city's public square — down Euclid Avenue, Ninth Street, Prospect Avenue, 14th Street; up Euclid and Ninth Street again to Sixth Street and, finally, to City Hall for a special ceremony on the steps.

Judge James B. Ruhl, chairman of the Balto Committee, gave a short but moving speech that is still quoted today. "The dog is man's best friend," the judge said solemnly. "A dog's love is akin to a mother's love. He is man's last friend when the cloud of misfortune hangs over him. And he is to be found watching at his master's grave when the last friend has departed."

With those words, the good feeling breached its banks. Tears spilled over, rolled down fat little cheeks and even stubbly beards. The huge crowd thought about how much mankind owed the humble dog for all its help down through the ages. It was a debt that never could really be repaid. But one city could help seven dogs — could take good care of them and give them the comfortable retirements they deserved. The great heart of Cleveland, composed of all the little hearts of the people, opened wide and welcomed the dogs home.

Chapter Nineteen
The Dogs Receive
Their First Visitors

Balto Day in Cleveland became Balto Weekend. On Sunday, the day after the parade, thousands of well-wishers visited the zoo to meet the dogs.

The team's new outdoor pen wasn't yet ready, so the dogs received visitors in their basement digs — after a hearty breakfast of a pound of raw meat each and veggies. People who hadn't visited the zoo in years climbed out of bed like sleepwalkers, heading to the zoo almost without thinking, as if they had been programmed. They knew only that the zoo was the place to be on Sunday, and that they wanted to go there. And Balto and his six teammates were the star attractions, more popular than any of the other animals.

People who had only glimpsed the dogs from the parade's sidelines wanted to gaze fully into the dogs' handsome faces, peer into their intensely alive, bright eyes, bask in their special magic, which was the magic of their breed, really. (Huskies, you may recall, were still rare in the 48 states that then made up America.) But there was something else, too.

The dogs were like proud veterans home from a long war after many battles: the dangerous serum run, their grueling travels across the country, their long prison sentence in the dime museum. These huskies were more than heroes; they were survivors: strong, resilient, deserving of the highest praise.

Over eight hours, 15,000 people swept through the zoo's turnstiles like a great wave. Al Kintzel, the dogs' newly appointed keeper, directed the steady flow of human traffic in and out of the basement, gently cautioning, "Watch your step." Thousands of children, their eyes round with wonder like pilgrims inching toward a shrine, led parents and grandparents down the narrow stone steps. "Come on," they pleaded, tugging the sleeves of the adults in a most unpilgrimlike way. "I want to see Balto."

None were disappointed. "Wynken, Blynken and Nod," mused one small boy, who like many of the children, wished with all his heart he could take the dogs home. "I like Balto, Alaska Slim and Old Moctoc better."

At noon, the bottleneck was halted and the dogs were taken outside for some fresh air and a short, brisk run. Then they trotted down to the basement and allowed themselves to be admired for four more hours — until the zoo finally closed for the day. Old Moctoc snoozed a bit, but that was to be expected. Once or twice, Balto was brought close to the children to be petted and hugged. For dinner, the dogs each ate two biscuits, which was all they wanted. They were too tired to eat more and quickly fell asleep.

Courtesy of Special Collections, Cleveland University Library.

Chapter Twenty
Moving Day

Within days, the zoo opened a new outdoor exhibit: the team's new home! Shaped like a half-moon — or a wide smile — the fenced-in area was grassed and had a large, leafy shade tree as shelter against the bright Midwestern sun and rain. Size-wise, it was considered generous for a dog yard then: 100 feet in diameter and 50 feet wide (a third the length of a football field and a third the width). The pen was described in a news story as "proper shelter," a place where the dogs could live contentedly while on display.

They did. After the hoopla died down, the dogs continued to be one of the zoo's most popular exhibits, which was un-usual: Many zoos display wild dogs, such as dingoes or wolves, but none display domestic dogs — the kind that humans, over thousands of years, have turned into loyal pets. You don't see Labs or poodles in zoos, do you? You don't see them today, and you didn't see them in the 1920s. Cleveland's Balto exhibit was something unique in the annals, or records, of zoo history. A zoo was simply an unusual place for domestic dogs to live, but then these dogs had led unusual lives.

But the zoo exhibit was no freak show, no cheap display of "animal oddities." It was the dogs' retirement home, a place where they could play, sleep, eat and rest — in relative peace and quiet and surrounded by nature.

There were fewer exhibits then, mostly animals of local origin, including raccoon, foxes, bears, deer and a flock of Canada geese. Prairie dogs and ostrich were among the few exotic species. The deer were nearby, but there were no other animal species that the dogs could see — just trees, flowers, landscaped walkways and lush parkland. The dogs were happy, especially in winter, when it snowed and they got to pull their sled around Brookside Park. They went on several runs a week. Balto remained the No. 1 leader, but Fox sometimes got to lead, too.

Chapter Twenty One
A Great Heart Falters

In 1930, the dogs watched a huge construction project unfold like a magic trick: the Fulton Road Bridge. The zoo grounds were cradled in a narrow valley and, with more and more people driving cars, an overpass was needed to ease traffic and connect Fulton Road to the rest of the city.

Soon, people were driving over the valley instead of around it, taking them right over the far end of the zoo — and practically over the dogs' heads. For the curious dogs, the sights and sounds of the bridge being built and later, the endless whiz of cars, were a constant source of entertainment.

But the dogs were growing old. Each day, they played a little less and slept a little more until one by one, they died. By March 1933 — six years after the team's arrival at the zoo — only two dogs were left. Gone were Old Moctoc, the team's oldest member, with his wizened, wolf-like features, and Fox, the second-in-command after Balto in the dogs' heyday of sled runs. Gone, too — but not forgotten by the children of Cleveland — were Alaska Slim, Billy and Tillie, with her gleaming gray-and-cream-colored coat. Only Sye and Balto remained, two old comrades, sharing their last days under a shade tree in the moon-shaped pen.

But Balto's great heart was faltering. Now age 11, he was partly deaf, partly blind and barely able to move his back legs, which were inflamed with arthritis and stiff. It was clear to his keeper, Captain Curley Wilson, that Balto was dying, breathing with difficulty and sleeping so much that every time he drifted off, Curly wondered whether he would awake.

Finally, a kind veterinarian, Dr. R.R. Powell, offered to ease Balto's last days — to make him more comfortable and gently end his struggle. Curley accepted, and Balto was carefully moved to Dr. Powell's animal hospital — just in time. He was slipping further beyond reach by the hour, plummeting through silence and whiteness into a comforting cloud castle of unconsciousness.

The distressing news was reported in the papers, setting off an avalanche of phone calls from children to the zoo. "How's Balto?" "Is he suffering?" "How's Sye doing?" they wanted to know. Zoo officials assured the children that Balto was in good hands.

But Sye was lonely, moaning and howling inconsolably as if a full moon had emerged from behind a cloud. He paced back and forth in his pen like an agitated prisoner and barely touched his food. Sye was alone. Given his keen husky instincts, he must have known that his lifelong companion would never return.

Dr. Powell insisted on caring for Balto free of charge. He was glad to be of assistance, even honored to be entrusted with caring for the dog during his final hours. On Tuesday, March 14, the veterinarian injected the comatose, or nearly lifeless, dog with a drug to hasten his slide into peace. Balto died a few hours later — at 2:15 p.m. Sye had lost his best friend, and the people of Cleveland had lost a beloved pet.

Chapter Twenty Two
The Aftermath

The next day, an autopsy showed that Balto had died of old age. This made everyone feel a little better, knowing that there was nothing that could have been done — that it had just been Balto's time to die. All the dog's organs appeared to be normal except for his bladder, which was greatly enlarged. Balto lived to a "ripe age for a dog," said Captain Wilson. In human years, he was "like a man past 70," he said. Balto had had a long and interesting life, especially for a dog, and his last years had been good ones. Now, it was time to say goodbye.

But Balto's many friends at the zoo couldn't. Neither could the people of Cleveland. So the husky's still-impressive body was lovingly stuffed and mounted by a staff taxidermist at the Cleveland Museum of Natural History.

When he was done, Balto looked alive. His beautiful black fur was thick and glossy. The mount had poise, presence. Perhaps because the mount was created with so much feeling, it exuded something special: the old Balto magic, the unmistakable approximation of Balto's charisma and spirit. The mount wasn't disgusting or creepy. It was beautiful, like Balto.

"Instead of the vigorous pulsing body which took hope to Nome," Balto's fur now was "stretched life-like" over an artificial form, the *Plain Dealer* wrote in an editorial.

The mount was all that Cleveland had left of the great dog, and the museum planned to take good care of it. It was a way to keep the story of Balto alive for posterity, so that he would never be forgotten.

Almost seven decades later, he hasn't been.

Chapter Twenty Three
The Epilogue

The year after Balto died, Sye, then 17, died of "bladder stones and complications," the *Plain Dealer* reported, and the zoo's dog pen was torn down. Of the zoo's seven huskies, Sye was the only one to breed — he impregnated a German police dog. Hmm. How did that happen? No one any longer knows, if anyone ever did. Perhaps Sye broke out of the dog yard one day, saw a police dog that had strayed onto the zoo grounds, and made a beeline for her. Perhaps a zoo keeper or other member of the zoo staff arranged a secret tryst between Sye and the police dog to ensure that at least one of the seven dogs' genes were passed on. (Such an anonymous match-maker could not have chosen Balto as Seppala had had him neutered.) Two weeks before Sye died, the German police dog gave birth to five pups, though only one survived. What happened to it? No one knows, but we like to think that a little part of Sye lives on somewhere.

In 1934, the same year Sye died, fire broke out in Nome, and the tiny Alaska town burned to the ground. It was rebuilt, and today 4,021 people live there. Every winter, the town's residents turn out to watch the winner of the 1,150-mile Iditarod Trail Sled Dog Race cross the finish line downtown. The race honors the 1925 serum run by following part of the same trail that Balto and his fellow dogs took.

In 1929, the party decade ended with a loud pop when the stock market crashed. The value of individual stock shares plummeted, in many cases to way below what people had paid

for them. Many Americans lost most or even all of their invest‑
ments. Banks, factories and shops closed, leaving millions of
people jobless and penniless. It was one of the scariest times in
U.S. history. Then in 1932, President Franklin D. Roosevelt was
elected. In a moving inaugural speech, he said: "We have nothing
to fear but fear itself." FDR — as the president was called — had
many new ideas for how to help people and fix the economy.
The reforms were pushed through Congress in just 100 days.
The "New Deal" with the American people provided help to the
poor and created thousands of jobs. A virtual army of Americans
went to work for the government building highways, parks and
zoos. Many writers and artists were given jobs, too. The country
pulled together and the economy began to stabilize. But it took
World War II to end the Great Depression, which affected most
of the world. In the late 1930s, Germany and Japan attacked
many countries in Europe and Asia. To fight the two enemies
to world peace, the United States and its Allies had to greatly
increase their production of weapons and other war materials.
The war effort provided millions of people with jobs.

In 1930, the American Kennel Club recognized the Siberian
Husky as a distinct breed.

Seppala's legendary dog, Togo, spent the sunset of his life
in Poland Spring, Maine, with Elizabeth Ricker, Seppala's good
friend and a champion sled-dog racer. In 1928, Ricker wrote
Togo's Fireside Reflections, a charming work of fiction based on
fact. In it, Togo stretches out luxuriously before a crackling fire
in a cozy New England home and tells his life's story to two
rapt children. "My mother was like the princess in your stories,"
Togo begins. "She was beautiful and gentle and everyone who
knew her loved her, but she was sometimes very sad and lonely,
I think, for she was a long way from home. She had come from
the Kolyma River in Siberia, and there were few other dogs in
Alaska from there." A few copies of the book still can be found
in libraries, and occasionally one goes up for auction on the
Internet. (In 1999, one copy sold for $128!)

Togo fathered many puppies at Ricker's kennels. After he
died in 1929 at 16, his body, too, was mounted and displayed

— for 20 years at the Peabody Museum of Natural History at Yale University. Seppala visited Togo there in 1960, when he was in his 80s. "I never had a better dog than Togo," he said. "His stamina, loyalty and intelligence could not be improved upon. Togo was the best dog that ever traveled the Alaska trail."

In 1964, the mount was acquired by the Shelburne Museum in Shelburne, Vermont. But it was unprotected and over time was worn nearly threadbare from visitors' petting. In 1979, the mount was placed in storage, where it languished for several years — until a newspaper story sparked a campaign by some Alaskans to get Togo back. Children, officials and dog clubs wrote letters to members of Congress, demanding that Togo be returned to the state of his birth. In 1983, a deal was worked out and the museum gave Togo to the Iditarod Trail Committee. Today, the mount can be seen in a glass case in a dimly lit room at Iditarod race headquarters in Wasilla. It has seen better days. The Peabody Museum still has Togo's bones, which also were mounted. The skeleton is in storage.

Also in 1928, the fearless explorer, Roald Amundsen, disappeared on a flight to the North Pole to rescue his old adversary, Umberto Nobile, whose plane had crashed on the ice. The brash Italian aviator eventually was rescued, but not by Amundsen, whose own plane plunged into the sea.

And what became of the other characters in our story? Sol Lesser had a long and successful career as a major Hollywood producer. He produced 117 feature films, including 16 "Tarzan" movies. In 1951, he won an Oscar for *Kon-Tiki*, a documentary about the famous raft expedition made in 1947 from Peru to Polynesia by Thor Heyerdahl, a Norwegian zoologist and adventurer. In 1960, Lesser won a humanitarian award for his support of theatrical and movie industry causes. He died in 1980 at age 90.

In 1950, Gunnar Kaasen left Nome and moved to Seattle, where he died a decade later at age 78. The author was unable to locate any of his relatives. In his obituary, he was described as a former miner and civil engineer.

Leonhard Seppala died in Seattle in 1967 at age 90. His wife,

Constance, scattered his ashes along the Iditarod Trail. He is still a legend in Alaska, though his name is not well known in the Lower 48.

Cleveland businessman George Kimble quietly moved to New York, but his thread in this story has been lost. The author could not learn when or where he died.

Sam Houston, the owner of the dime museum, toured the West with a live gorilla and managed a circus, not necessarily in that order. In the late 1930s, he bought three railroad baggage cars and filled them with a collection of odd objects: wax figures, a one-man Japanese submarine, a dead, mounted, two-headed calf; a saddle that allegedly once belonged to Pancho Villa, the famous Mexican bandit and revolutionary. (The saddle had a rear view mirror so that Villa could see any enemies riding up behind him.) Houston would hitch the cars to a train and the train would pull the strange exhibit from town to town. His last known venture was a dime museum with a "wishing well" inside. The author does not know when Houston died. He is said to have been a handsome man, and lived in a hotel in Los Angeles.

Frederick George Richard Roth died in 1944 after a long career during which he created many beautiful large and small animal sculptures which still grace many American buildings, parks and museums.

In 1998, Cody McGinn, a third-grader in Palmer, Alaska, with the help of his teacher, launched a campaign to get Balto back, and the Alaska Legislature officially asked the Cleveland Museum of Natural History to return the mount. The museum declined, but agreed to lend the mount to the Anchorage Museum of History and Art for a three-month exhibit. It did — for the 1999 Iditarod race — and the show was a huge success. When Cody heard Balto's full story and all that he had suffered after the serum run, he told this author: "Cleveland helped save him, so he belongs to both sides. Maybe we could share him." The author disagrees and feels Balto rightly belongs to Cleveland. But she hopes the museum will continue to let the mount travel to other U.S. cities so as many children as possible can see it.

Today, 67 years after Balto's death, the mount still exudes something magical and powerful. Balto's shiny black fur has faded to mahogany, the natural effect of air and light exposure, and his white "socks" are now light gray. But the fur is still thick and lustrous, and the body is strong and muscular. Balto's eyes are now glass beads, but they shine through the glass case that contains the mount in a transfixing way. They look very real, and the gaze is alert and dignified. The mount is displayed each year for several weeks around the time of the Iditarod, along with an 8-minute video of old film clips, including one showing Kaasen, Balto and the rest of the team in Nome shortly after the serum run. Another shows Dr. Curtis Welch injecting a diphtheria-stricken child with serum at Nome's small hospital in 1925. Still another shows Seppala and his dogs, including Togo, arriving by ship in Seattle. The museum's annual Balto display is wonderful! It changes slightly from year to year as the museum acquires new Balto memorabilia and details of the story. The museum hopes to someday find a copy of Lesser's 20-minute re-enactment of the serum run.

Nothing could be learned about the fates of the five huskies that are unnamed in this story. One or more dogs may have died in the dime museum, or on the vaudeville tour. Of those that were sold, at least one reportedly produced offspring. The author would like to think that some dogs in America today carry the genes of at least some of Balto's teammates.

Balto's statue still overlooks Central Park. So many children have climbed on the larger-than-life bronze dog and hugged it so fiercely for so many years that parts have been rubbed golden, while the rest has turned bluish green with verdigris, a natural chemical residue that forms on bronze. The statue is between 66th Street and 67th Street on the east side of the park. According to the official *Guide to Manhattan's Outdoor Sculpture*, it is New York's only statue commemorating a dog. (Unfortunately, the guide incorrectly states that Balto died as a result of the serum run!)

In Cleveland, nothing at all remains of the old Brookside Zoo — not one original exhibit — and the zoo's name has been changed to Cleveland Metroparks Zoo. The oldest exhibit still standing — Monkey Island — was built in 1936 — three years after Balto's death. The Fulton Road Bridge is crumbling — so dangerously that a safety net has been draped from the bridge to prevent any loose chunks from falling on the heads of zoo visitors. The team's sled has mysteriously disappeared, along with all its collars, food dishes and water bowls and six of the seven harnesses. The one remaining harness is on display at the Wolf Wilderness gift shop. Was it Balto's? No one knows.

Happily, Balto and Togo have been reunited, at least symbolically. Bronze statues of the two famous huskies have been placed outside the Wolf Wilderness exhibit center, which looks like an old trapper's cabin.

Balto sits erect; Togo is lying down. They seem be looking up at a wooded ridge slightly behind and above them — at the very real gray wolves that live there and seem often to be looking back at them.

The End

Sources

Information on Balto and the other characters in this book was drawn from a wide variety of sources, including old newspaper stories, letters, books, magazines, press releases, film clips and interviews with surviving relatives and acquaintances. Many of the sources, or references to them, were found in the Cleveland Museum of Natural History's Balto archives, where the research for this book began. In cases where information from one source conflicted with another, the author used that which she thought more credible. Here are some of the sources:

The Race to Nome by Kenneth A. Ungermann; Harper & Row, Publishers, 1963

Seppala: Alaskan Dog Driver by Elizabeth M. Ricker; Little, Brown, and Company, 1930

Seppala's Saga of the Sled Dog by Raymond Thompson, self-published sometime in the 1970s. Existing copies are very rare.

Togo's Fireside Reflections by Elizabeth M. Ricker; Lewiston Journal Printshop, 1928

Togo, The Hero Dog by Barbara L. Narendra, *Discovery, The Magazine of the Yale Peabody Museum of Natural History*, Volume 24, Number 2, 1993

The Complete Siberian Husky by Lorna D. Demidoff and Michael Jennings; Howell Book House, Inc., New York 1978

Roald Amundsen: A Saga of the Polar Seas by J. Alvin Kugelmass; Julian Messner, Inc., 1955

Nansen: The Explorer as Hero by Roland Huntford; Barnes & Noble Books, 1998

The Last Place on Earth: Scott and Amundsen's Race to the South Pole by Roland Huntford; Modern Library, New York, 1983

Fifty Years of Vaudeville, 1895-1945 by Ernest Short; Eyre & Spottiswoode London, 1946

Once Upon a Stage, the Merry World of Vaudeville by Charles and Louise Samuels; Dodd, Mead & Co., New York, 1974

LEISURE and Entertainment in AMERICA by Donna R. Braden; Henry Ford Museum & Greenfield Village, Dearborn, Michigan, 1988

Freak Show by Robert Bogdan; The University of Chicago Press, 1988

American History in 100 Nutshells by Tad Tuleja; Fawcett Columbine, 1992

New York: A Documentary by Ric Burns

The Cleveland Plain Dealer, New York Times, Seattle Times, Los Angeles Times, Detroit Free Press, United Press International, Nome Nugget, Siberian Husky Club News and *Northern Dog News.*

Mount Rainier National Park Official Web Site